George Peck Eckman

Controversial Elements in Lucretius

A Thesis for the Doctorate in Philosophy

George Peck Eckman

Controversial Elements in Lucretius
A Thesis for the Doctorate in Philosophy

ISBN/EAN: 9783337277291

Printed in Europe, USA, Canada, Australia, Japan

Cover: Foto ©Thomas Meinert / pixelio.de

More available books at **www.hansebooks.com**

Controversial Elements in Lucretius

A THESIS

FOR THE

Doctorate in Philosophy

—BY—

GEORGE P. ECKMAN

APPROVED BY THE FACULTY OF THE GRADUATE SCHOOL OF THE NEW YORK UNIVERSITY, 1897

NEW YORK
1899

Table of Contents.

INTRODUCTION.

(A) CONTEMPORARY INTEREST IN EPICUREANISM.

Character of the period. Causes of the apparent neglect of Lucretius by his contemporaries. Influence of Epicureanism upon cultivated Romans. Reasons for Cicero's comparative silence regarding Lucretius. Recognition of the poet by later generations.

(B) A PRELIMINARY QUESTION.

To what extent did Lucretius pursue original investigations? The poet's devotion to Epicurus. Evidences of servile imitation. Marks of independent treatment of physical phenomena. No extreme position tenable. Divisions of the present discussion.

I. PHILOSOPHERS WITH WHOM LUCRETIUS CONTENDS AMICABLY.

Respects for early physicists. The main contention,

1. Empedocles. Object of Lucretius' admiration. Internal evidence that Lucretius studied the works of Empedocles. Hallier's proofs. Similarity of literary style. Rhetorical imitations. Doctrinal agreement. Resemblances in explanations of physical phenomena. Unquestioned indebtedness of Lucretius. Hostility to Empedocles as representative physicist designating one or more substances primordial matter. Various points of conflict. Void and motion. Incompetent *primordia.* Fallibility of the senses. Mortality of the soul. Teleology.

2. Anaxagoras. Evidence of high esteem of Epicurus for Anaxagoras. Common ground occupied by Anaxagoras and Atomists. General lines of divergence. Sympathy of Lucretius with Anaxagoras. Instances in proof. The doctrine of the *homoeomeria* the real issue between Lucretius and Anaxagoras. The theory expounded. Objections of Lucretius. Void ignored. Infinite divisibility of body. Defective *primordia.* Secondary qualities in primitive matter. *Minima.* A pair of dilemmas.

3. Democritus. The obligation of Epicurus to the philosopher of Abdera. Ingratitude of the former. The more commendable spirit of Lucretius. Eulogistic lines. Traces of the pressure of Democritus upon Lucretius. Harmony of general principles. The doctrine of emanations. The *summum bonum*. The sexual passion. Earthquakes. Imitations of Democritus. The extent of Lucretius' acquaintance with his writings. Chief doctrinal disagreement. Atomic declination. Free-will. Arguments of Epicurus and Lucretius. Minor occasions of controversy. Infinity of number and shapes of atoms. Constitution of the soul. Origin of verbal designations. The rising of the Nile. The gods.

II. PHILOSOPHERS TOWARD WHOM LUCRETIUS IS HOSTILE.
The censoriousness of Epicurus emulated by Lucretius.
1. Heraclitus. Alone denounced by name. Taunt of obscurity. Avowed reason for the animosity of Lucretius toward Heraclitus the latter's assertion that fire is the original essence from which everything has been derived. Order of Lucretius' arguments. Is the poet's treatment of Heraclitus just? Character of his elemental fire. Hypothesis of condensation and rarefaction. Void eliminated. Change by extinction. Doctrine of the senses. Transmutation of primitive matter. Heraclitus and the Stoics.

2. The Stoics. Antagonism of Lucretius an inherited passion. Mutual calumnies of the Stoics and Epicureans. Irrepressible conflict on the subject of nature. Specific points of controversy. Properties and accidents. Corporeality and reality. Elemental fire. The structure and course of the universe. Infinity of space and matter. Theory of centripetal force. Immortality and divinity of the world. Cosmic systems. The world as a living organism. Destructibility of the world. Theological positions. The character and functions of deity. Stoic ideas of creation and providence incompatible with the supreme repose and happiness of the gods. Likewise disproved by the imperfections of creation. The desire to deliver men from the fear of divine interference the basic reason for Lucretius' argument against Providence, Only valid ground for scientific study. Final cause denied. True philosophy of the gods. Myth of Kybele. Epicureans and Stoics in relation to popular religion. Stern denunciation of prevalent superstition. Apparent inconsistency of Lucretius.

BIBLIOGRAPHY

OF THE CHIEF WORKS CONSULTED IN THIS DISCUSSION.

DIOGENES LAERTIUS—*De Vitis Philosophorum*, Tauchnitz, Leipsic, 1895.

CICERO, MARCUS TULLIUS—*De Natura Deorum, De Finibus, etc.*, Teubner, Leipsig, 1894.

RITTER ET PRELLER—*Historia Philosophiae Graecae*, 7th Edition, Gothae, 1888.

MUNRO, H. A. J.—*T. Lucreti Cari De Rerum Natura*, Text, Notes, etc., 4th Ed., Cambridge, 1893.

ZELLER, E.—*Pre-Socratic Philosophy; Stoics, Epicureans and Sceptics*, London, 1892.

USENER, HERMANN—*Epicurea*, Leipsig, 1887.

TEUFFEL, W. S.—*History of Roman Literature*, London, 1873.

FAIRBANKS, ARTHUR—*The First Philosophers of Greece*, New York, 1898.

SELLAR, W. Y.—*Roman Poets of the Republic*, 3d Edition, Oxford, 1889.

HALLIER, AEMILIUS—*Lucreti Carmina e Fragmentis Empedoclis Adumbrata*, Jena, 1857.

MOMMSEN, THEODOR—*History of Rome*, New York, 1875.

MASSON, JOHN—*The Atomic Theory of Lucretius*, London, 1884.

CORRIGENDA.

P. 8, note 2, read *plurimis* instead of *plurimus;* consulere not *considere*.
P. 9, line 4, read *Catius Insuber*.
P. 26, line 26, read καίτοι instead of καἰτοι.
P. 29, line 13, read 'Ἐμπεδοκλεῖ; ἀναγκαῖον for αναγκαῖον.
P. 30, line 3, read *queunt* instead of *quent*.
P. 31, line 9, read στείροις instead of στείροις.
    line 22, read γυμνοὶ instead of γμυνοὶ.
    line 23, read πενητεύοντα instead of πενητευοντα.
P. 32, line 22, read φησὶ instead of φηοὶ.
P. 38, line 27, read τὸ ὁμοιομερές instead of τὸ ὁμοιομερεῖα.
P. 46, line 27, read *deprauare* instead of *depruare*.
P. 68, line 10, read βίβλοις instead of βίβλιοις.
P. 75, line 7, read πρῶτον instead of πρῶτων.
P. 81, line 1, read *nunquam* instead of *nemquam;* remove period after *Chrysippam*.
    line 2, read *vocabat* instead of *vocebat*.
P. 82, note 2, read *Praefatio* instead of *Prefatio*.
P. 90, line 18, read τούτων instead of τούων.
P. 103, line 11, read πρόληψις instead of πρόληφις.

CONTROVERSIAL ELEMENTS
IN
LUCRETIUS.

INTRODUCTION.

Contemporary Interest in Epicureanism.

It cannot be denied that the poem of Lucretius failed to awaken any marked interest until long after its publication. The almost unbroken silence of his contemporaries regarding him is significant of the comparative indifference with which his production was received. The reasons for this neglect are various and not far to seek. In the first place the moment was inopportune for the appearance of such a work. "It was composed in that hapless time when the rule of the oligarchy had been overthrown and that of Caesar had not yet been established, in the sultry years during which the outbreak of the civil war was awaited with long and painful suspense."[1] The poet betrays his solicitude for the welfare of his country at this crisis in the introduction of his work, in which he invokes the aid of Venus in persuading Mars to command peace—

> *Effice ut interea fera moenera militiai*
> *Per maria ac terras omnis sopita quiescant*[2]—

and acknowledges that his attention is diverted from literary labors by the exigencies of the state :

> *Nam neque nos agere hoc patriai tempore iniquo*
> *Possumus aequo animo nec Memmi clara propago*
> *Talibus in rebus communi desse saluti.*[3]

Munro believes these lines were written toward the close of 695, when Caesar as consul had formed his coalition with Pompey and when there was almost a reign of terror.[4] The reflection of a state of

---

[1] Mommsen, *Hist. Rome*, IV, p. 698 (Eng. Tr.).
[2] I, 29, 30.
[3] I. 41-43.
[4] Munro, *Lucretius*, II. p. 30.

tumult and peril is equally obvious in the opening verses of the second book, where the security of the contemplative life is contrasted with the turbulence of a political and military career.[1] Particularly significant are the lines :

> *Si non forte tuas legiones per loca campi*
> *Fervere cum videas belli simulacra cientis,*
> *Subsidiis magnis et ecum vi constabilitas,*
> *Ornatasque armis statuas pariterque animatas,*
> *His tibi tum rebus timefactae religiones*
> *Effugiunt animo pavide ; mortisque timores*
> *Tum vacuum pectus lincunt curaque solutum,*
> *Fervere cum videas classem lateque vagari.*[2]

It can readily be appreciated that a period of such fermentation and alarm would afford opportunity for philosophic study to those alone who were able to retire from political excitements to private leisure and quiet. Moreover the very characteristics of the Epicurean philosophy would recommend it chiefly to persons of this description. Participation in public life was distinctly discouraged by the school of Epicurus, who regarded the realm of politics as a world of tumult and trouble, wherein happiness—the chief end of life—was almost, if not quite, impossible. They counselled entering the arena of public affairs only as an occasional and disagreeable necessity, or as a possible means of allaying the discontent of those to whom the quiet of a private life was not wholly satisfactory.[3] Such instruction, though phrased in the noble hexameters of a Lucretius, was scarcely calculated to enjoy immediate popularity in the stirring epoch of a fast hurrying revolution.[4]

---

[1] Sellar, *Roman Poets of the Republic*, p. 290.

[2] II, 40-47. "Caesar after his consulship remained with his army for three months before Rome, and was bitterly attacked by Memmius. Does Lucretius here allude to Caesar ? " Munro, II, p. 122.

[3] Zeller, *Stoics, Epicureans and Sceptics*, p. 491, 3, 6.

[4] "In consequence of his mode of thought and writing being so averse to his own time and directed to a better future, the poet received little attention in his own age." Teuffel, *Hist. Rom. Lit.* I, 201 (Eng. Tr.). "It (Epicureanism) arose in a state of society and under circumstances widely different from the social and political condition of the last phase of the Roman Republic." Sellar, *Roman Poets of the Republic*, p. 357.

A somewhat ingenious, but unsuccessful, attempt has been made to account for the indifference with which Lucretius was treated on the ground of his assault upon the doctrine of the future life. It has been suggested that as the enmity of the Christian writers was early called down upon his head for this cause, he was likewise whelmed under a conspiracy of silence on the part of his Roman contemporaries and successors" for the same reason.[1] But so general was the skepticism of his age on this question, that it is scarcely credible that the publication of his views could have seriously scandalized the cultured classes who read his lines. The same judgment will hold true with reference to the entire attitude of Lucretius toward the traditional religion. It is a sufficient answer to the theory that his infidelity created antipathy toward him to record the fact that Julius Caesar, than whom no more pronounced free-thinker lived in his day, was, despite his skepticism, *pontifex maximus* of the Roman commonwealth, and did not hesitate to declare in the presence of the Senate that the immortality of the soul was a vain delusion.[2] That he represented in these heretical opinions the position of many of the foremost persons of the period is the testimony of contemporary literature.

Shall we not find the better reason for the apparent neglect of Lucretius in the era immediately following the issue of his poem in the fact that there was no public at this juncture for the study of Greek philosophy clothed in the Latin language? Cicero, who devoted himself with the zeal of a patriot to the creation of a philosophical literature in his native tongue, complained of the scant courtesy paid to his efforts. *Non eram nescius, Brute, cum, quae summis ingeniis exquisitaque doctrina philosophi Graeco sermone tractavissent, ea Latinis literis mandaremus, fore ut hic noster labor in varias reprchensiones incurreret. Nam quibusdam, et iis quidem non admodum indoctis, totum hoc displicet, philosophari. Quidam autem non tam id reprehendunt, si remissius agatur, sed tantum studium tamque multam operam ponendam in eo non arbitrabantur. Erunt etiam, et ii quidem eruditi Graecis litteris, contemnentes Latinas, qui se dicant in Graecis legendis operam malle consumere. Postremo aliquos futuros suspicor, qui me ad alias litteras vocent,*

---

[1] This is the view advanced by R. T. Tyrrell of the University of Dublin. See his *Latin Poetry*, p. 74. (Houghton, Mifflin & Co., N. Y., 1895).
[2] Merivale, *History of the Romans*, II, p. 354.

genus hoc scribendi, etsi sit elegans, personae tamen et dignitatis esse negent.[1] Yet this work, as he explains in his *De Divinatione*,[2] was undertaken with the commendable purpose of benefitting his countrymen. He anticipated with delight the advantages which would accrue to them when his researches were complete. *Magnificum illud etiam Romanisque hominibus gloriosum, ut Graecis de philosophia litteris non egeant.*[3] And later he reaped his reward in an awakened interest in the subjects of his studious inquiries. But he was compelled in the beginning to cultivate a sentiment in behalf of those investigations. Lucretius addressed himself to an unsympathetic public, and was likewise required to wait for applause until a more appreciative generation rose up to do him honor.

Yet it must not be supposed that Epicureanism exercised a feeble influence over the thought of cultivated Romans in this period of their history. The very theme which engaged the genius of Lucretius had also employed the energies of predecessors and contemporaries. Among attempts of this character were the *De Rerum Natura* of Egnatius, which appeared somewhat earlier than the work of Lucretius; the *Empedoclea* of Sallustius mentioned by Cicero in the much discussed passage relating to Lucretius; and a metrical production entitled *De Rerum Natura* by Varro.[4] Commentaries on the principles of Epicureanism had also been extant for some time. Chief among the authors of such compositions was Amafinius who preceded Lucretius by nearly a century. Our knowledge of him is mainly derived from Cicero, who says: *C. Amafinius exstitit dicens cuius libris editis commota multitudo contulit se ad eam potissimum disciplinam.*[5] Rabirius is also mentioned by the same author as belonging to that class of writers, *Qui nulla arte adhibita de rebus ante oculos positis vol-*

---

[1] *De Finibus*, I, 1.
[2] *Quaerenti mihi multumque et diu cogitanti, quanam re possem prodesse quam plurimus, ne quando intermitterem considere reipublicae, nulla maior occurrebat, quam si optimarum artium vias traderem meis civibus; quod conpluribus iam libris me arbitror consecutum.* . . . *Quod enim munus rei publicae adferre maius meliusve possumus, quam si docemus atque erudimus iuventutem? his praesertim moribus atque temporibus, quibus ita prolapsa est,* etc. II, 1, 2.
[3] *De Divinatione.* II, 2.
[4] Sellar, *Roman Poets of the Republic*, p. 278.
[5] *Acad.* I. 2. 5.

gari sermone disputant.[1] Rabirius indulged in a popular treatment of philosophy and covered much the same ground as Amafinius. Another contributor to the literature of Epicureanism whom Cicero records in no complimentary way is Catius—*Catius insuber, Epicureus, qui nuper est mortuus, quae ille Gargettius et iam ante Democritus εἴδωλα, hic spectra nominat.*[2]

The interest in this school of philosophy among Romans of the time of Lucretius is further apparent in the prominence which certain Epicurean teachers attained. Conspicuous among them is Zeno the Sidonian, whose lectures Cicero in company with Atticus had attended on the occasion of his first visit to Athens, 79 to 78 B.C., whom he calls the prince of Epicureans in his *De Natura Deorum*,[3] and whose instruction is doubtless liberally embodied in Cicero's discussions of the system of Epicureanism.[4] Contemporary with Zeno was Phaedrus,[5] who had achieved distinction in Athens and Rome, in both of which places Cicero studied under his direction. Somewhat later Philodemus[6] of Gadara appeared in Rome, and is mentioned by Cicero as a learned and amiable man. The considerable body of writings bearing his name found in the *Volumina Herculanensia*[7] indicates his position among the philosophic instructors of his day. Scyro[8] a follower of Phaedrus, said to have been the teacher of Vergil; Patro[9] the successor of Phaedrus, who taught in Athens; and Pompilius Andronicus,[10] the grammarian who gave up his profession for the tenets of Epicurus, were eminent also at this period.

Partly as a result of the activity of these teachers of philosophy, and partly on account of the prevailing anxiety to arrive at some satisfactory scheme of life, the number of disciples of Epicurus steadily increased at this time, and included not a few illustrious names.

---

[1] *Tusc. Disp.*, IV, 6.
[2] *Ad Fam.*, XV, 16, 2.
[3] I, 21. Cf. *Diogenes Laertius*, X, 25.
[4] Ritter et Preller, *Hist. Phil. Graec.*, 447. a.
[5] *Ad Fam.*, XIII, 1.
[6] *De Fin.*, II, 35, 119.
[7] Ritter et Preller, *Hist. Phil. Graec.*, 447, a.
[8] *Ad. Fam.*, VI. 11.
[9] *Ad. Fam.*, XIII, 1. *Ad Attic*, V, 11.
[10] Zeller, *Stoics, Epicureans and Sceptics*, p. 414, 1.

These are known to us chiefly through the writings of Cicero,[1] who mentions T. Albutius, Velleius, C. Cassius, the well-known conspirator against Caesar, who may himself be classed among those who had lost confidence in the gods,[2] C. Vibius Pansa, Galbus, L. Piso, the patron of Philodemus, and L. Manlius Torquatus. Other notable personages are apparently regarded as Epicureans by Cicero, but grave doubts have been expressed concerning their real attitude toward the school. It is barely possible that Atticus may justly be denominated an Epicurean, for he calls the followers of Epicurus *nostri familiares*[3] and *condiscipuli*.[4] But his eclectic spirit would seem to forbid his classification with any single system, and Zeller[5] feels that neither he nor Asclepiades of Bithynia, a contemporary of Lucretius, who resided at Rome and was associated with Epicureans, can be regarded as genuine disciples of Epicurus.

The discussions of the Epicurean philosophy in *De Natura Deorum*, *De Finibus* and other works of Cicero evince the profound interest he had in the school, though his general attitude was one of unfriendliness. What reason, then, we may ask, can be given for his almost uninterrupted silence concerning Lucretius? The only reference we have to the poet in all Cicero's voluminous compositions occurs in a letter to his brother Quintus,[6] four months after the death of Lucretius, in which he says, *Lucretii poemata, ut scribis ita sunt: multis luminibus ingenii, multae etiam artis; sed cum veneris virum te putabo, si Sallustii Empedoclea legeris, hominem non putabo.* These words certainly imply that both Marcus and Quintus had read the poem, and many scholars accept the statement of Jerome in his additions to the Eusebian chronicle—*quos Cicero emendavit*—as applying to Marcus.[7] But if he was closely enough identified with the work of Lucretius to edit his manuscript, why in those writings wherein ample opportunity was afforded, did not Cicero mention his labors in the field of philosophy?

---

[1] Zeller, *Stoics, Epicureans and Sceptics*, p. 414, 3.
[2] Merivale, *Hist. Rom.*, II, pp. 352, 3.
[3] *De Fin.*, V, 1, 3.
[4] *Legg.*, I, 7, 21.
[5] *Stoics, Epicureans and Sceptics*, p. 415.
[6] *Ad Quintum*, II, 11.
[7] Munro (II, pp. 2-5) who discusses this question with his usual lucidity, inclines to the opinion that Jerome, following Suetonius, has indicated M. T. Cicero as the

This is a particularly pertinent inquiry in view of the fact that he does speak of Amafinius, Rabirius and Catius, as we have already observed, and that he devoted so much attention to the discussion of Epicurean principles. Munro answers this question by declaring that it was not Cicero's custom to quote from contemporaries, numerous as his citations are from the older poets and himself; that had he written on poetry as he did of philosophy and oratory, Lucretius would have undoubtedly occupied a prominent place in the work, and that more than once in his philosophical discussions Cicero unquestionably refers to Lucretius.[1] Munro is not alone in contending that the literary relations between Lucretius and Cicero were more or less intimate. Other critics have traced to Cicero's *Aratea* important lines in Lucretius, while many passages in Cicero closely resemble utterances of the poet. Martha quotes several remarkable parallels between *De Finibus* and various lines in Lucretius.[2] But it is argued on the other hand no less vigorously that didactic resemblances prove nothing, except that Lucretius and Cicero wrought from like sources their several Latinizations of Greek philosophy.

And herein there is suggested a possible explanation of Cicero's apparent indifference to the poet, whether he did him the favor of editing his verse or not. Cicero had made an earnest study of Greek philosophy long before the poem of Lucretius had been introduced to his notice. He had resorted to original authorities for information concerning Epicureanism. Zeno the Sidonian and Philodemus of Gadara, as already noted, had supplied him with much material. Everywhere in his philosophical works there is evidence that he regarded himself a sort of pioneer in this peculiar field of investigation,

---

editor of Lucretius, and that this was the real fact. Sellar, *Roman Poets of the Republic*, pp. 284-6, though suspending judgment does not deny the probability that M. T. Cicero performed this favor for Lucretius. Teuffel, *Hist. Rom. Lit.*, I, 201, 2, while expressing doubt concerning the evidence of Cicero's connection with the poem, declares that at any rate his "part was not very important, and it might almost seem that he was afraid of publishing a work of this kind." Prof. E. G. Sihler, N. Y. University, presents an argument of great force against the probability of Cicero's editorship. See Art. *Lucretius and Cicero*. *Transactions American Philological Association*, Vol. XXVIII, 1897.

[1] Munro, II, pp. 4, 5.
[2] M. Constant Martha, *Le Poeme de Lucrece*, quoted in Lee's *Lucretius*, p. xiv, 1.

and therefore deserving of the pre-eminence therein. He doubtless placed no importance upon any Latin writings beside his own which treated of this class of Greek culture. Indeed the references which he has made to persons engaged in an undertaking similar to his own are in no instance flattering. And Lucretius would only be esteemed by him a competitor in the same department of inquiry, who wrote in Latin verse instead of Latin prose.

Keeping these facts in mind the comparative silence of Cicero regarding Lucretius does not seem wholly incompatible with the theory of his editorship. He was himself an expositor of Epicurus—and that too of the hostile kind. He had "popularized the Epicurean doctrines in the bad sense of the word," and had thrown "a ludicrous color over many things which disappear when they are more seriously regarded."[1] Yet his opposition to the tenets of Epicurus would not preclude him from friendly association with many who professed them, and if asked to lend his name to the publication of Lucretius' verses, there could be no reason for withholding it. But if his antagonism to Epicureanism would lead him to speak against the doctrines of the poem, his admiration for the literary excellences of the work, as exhibited in his willingness to stand sponsor for its issue, would deter him from adverse criticism. Silence in such a case is the best evidence of friendship.

Mommsen[2] remarks that "Lucretius, although his poetical vigor as well as his art was admired by his cultivated contemporaries, yet remained—of late growth as he was—a master without scholars." But with increasing knowledge in what is best in Epicurus and a finer taste to appreciate the moral and literary virtues of Lucretius, subsequent generations gave ample recognition to the poet. Horace and Vergil were greatly influenced by him, particularly the latter, who is supposed to refer to Lucretius in the famous lines:

Felix qui potuit rerum cognoscere causas,
Atque metus omnes et inexorabile fatum,
Subiecit pedibus strepitumque Acherontis avari.[3]

---

[1] Lange, *History of Materialism*, I, p. 127 (Eng. Tr.).
[2] *Hist. Rome*, IV, p. 699.
[3] *Georgica*, II, 490-2.

Ovid pronounced words of high eulogy upon him:

> *Carmina sublimis tunc sunt peritura Lucreti*
> *Exitio terras cum dabit una dies.*[1]

The persistency of the Epicurean school of philosophy despite persecution and opposition down to the fourth century A.D. demonstrates its marvelous vitality and the almost deathless influence of the personality of Epicurus, whose single mind projected its grasp upon human thought throughout the whole existence of the sect. And not the least important agent in affecting this result, because of his almost idolatrous devotion to his master and the persuasive charm of his lines, was the poet Lucretius.

A Preliminary Question.

Before entering specifically upon an examination of the controversial elements in Lucretius, it will be important to inquire to what extent, if at all, the poet may be regarded an independent worker in the field he has chosen. One is impressed from the very beginning of his study of Lucretius with his profound moral earnestness. He is impelled by an absorbing passion to emancipate the human spirit from the terrors induced by the fear of death and the tyranny of superstition The constantly recurring application of his doctrines to the soul of the convert he hopes to make leads him into frequent repetitions of his constant aim, and should dissuade the student of Lucretius from attaching too much significance to his iterations elsewhere. In the scheme of the poem Epicurus is the savior of mankind, and Lucretius is his prophet. His entire energy seems to be devoted to the effort to render intelligible the process of Epicureanism in delivering men from irrational terrors. It is pertinent, therefore, to inquire whether it is probable that a man of such missionary zeal, who is consumed with a desire to propagate the theories of his master, would go out of his way to study other systems of philosophy. Is it not natural to infer from our knowledge of his characteristics that his acquaintance with rival schools of thought would be mainly, if not exclusively, derived from a perusal of Epicurus, and that he would deal with them from the traditional Epicurean point of view?

---

[1] *Amor.*, I. 15. 23.

In short are there any evidences that Lucretius engaged in independent research, when he undertook his exposition of philosophic doctrines? Scholars have arrayed themselves in extreme positions on this question. Woltyer[1] of Groningen represents one leading view, and maintains that Lucretius gave himself utterly to the Latinization of Epicurus. In support of this theory there are undeniably strong declarations in the poem. The exordia of Books III, V, VI, furnish ample marks of the almost slavish devotion of Lucretius to his master, and the whole poem breathes the same spirit. He professes only to imitate the peerless Epicurus:

> *E tenebris tantis tam clarum extollere lumen*
> *Qui primus potuisti inlustrans commoda vitae,*
> *Te sequor, o Graiae gentis decus, inque tuis nunc*
> *Ficta pedum pono pressis vestigia signis,*
> *Non ita certandi cupidus quam propter amorem*
> *Quod te imitari aveo.*[2]

He sees in him the highest human intelligence:

> *Qui genus humanum ingenio superavit et omnis*
> *Restincxit, stellas exortus ut aetherius sol.*[3]

His glory can never fade:

> *Cuius et extincti propter divina reperta*
> *Divolgata vetus iam ad caelum gloria fertur.*[4]

No honor can be too great for such a man:

> *Nam si, ut ipsa petit maiestas cognita rerum,*
> *Dicendum est, deus ille fuit, deus, inclyte Memmi.*[5]

Hence Lucretius will follow him explicitly:

> *Cuius ego ingressus vestigia dum rationes*
> *Persequor ac doceo dictis, quo quaeque creata*
> *Foedere sint.*[6]

---

[1] *Lucretii philosophia cum fontibus comparata*, Groningae, 1897.
[2] III, 1-5.
[3] III, 1043, 4.
[4] VI, 7, 8.
[5] V, 7, 8.
[6] V, 55-7.

It is apparent from the whole tenor of his production that Lucretius makes no claim to originality, his frequently avowed purpose being to disclose the method of Epicurus for the redemption of the race.

Moreover such a procedure is in perfect accord with the conventional usages of the Epicurean school, among the disciples of which there was mere dogmatic iteration of the original propositions of Epicurus. The κύριαι δόξαι, quoted by Diogenes Laertius,[1] were preserved expressly to be stored away in the memory of his adherents. So convinced was he of the value of his doctrines that he required not only these fundamental aphorisms, but whole summaries of his philosophy to be learned by rote.[2] His last words were: τῶν δογμάτων μεμνῆσθαι.[3] Such was the extravagant honor conferred upon Epicurus by his disciples that not only was his birthday observed by them during his lifetime, but the twentieth of each month was kept in celebration of him and Metrodorus.[4] Following the exhortation of a master to whom he was so deeply attached, Lucretius would be disposed to cling tenaciously to the expressed tenets of Epicurus, and would not be inclined to venture beyond them.

This tendency to adhere inflexibly to the teachings of their founder, was manifest in the remarkable sterility of production among later Epicureans, from the death of the master to the age of Cicero. This barrenness is particularly noticeable when contrasted with the fruitfulness of the Stoic school during the same period, as witness the names Cleanthes, Chrysippus, Boethus, Panaetius, Posidonius and others.[5] One reason for this unproductiveness lies in the fact that Epicurus, while he dogmatically laid down his atomistic physics, had at the same time a positive aversion to precise, specific, detailed study of natural phenomena, as it is best seen by a close examination of the letter to Pythocles, in which he summarily disposes of the questions relating to τὰ μετέωρα.[6] A survey of this presentation of the Epicurean doctrines on the facts of nature reveals a feeling that

---

[1] *Diog. Laer.*, X, 139-154.
[2] *Ib.*, 12, 35, 83, 85, 116.
[3] *Ib.*, 16.
[4] Zeller, *Epicureans, Stoics and Sceptics*, p. 418, 2.
[5] Ritter et Preller, *Hist. Phil. Graec.*, 422-26.
[6] *Diog. Laer.*, X, 84, sqq.

exact scientific knowledge is both impracticable and unnecessary. In a given case a variety of reasons may be offered in explanation, and the student is at liberty to take his preference.[1] Without an earnest purpose to study the facts of nature until they disclose the one and only interpretation for each phenomenon, there can be no real progress in science. The instances are not wanting in which a little deeper penetration into these facts of the universe on the part of Lucretius would have announced to the world in his day discoveries which were reserved to a much later period of time.

So convinced are some critics that Lucretius made no advance upon Epicurus, but contented himself with a servile Latinization of his Greek master's productions, that they even assert he obtained his account of the plague at Athens from Epicurus and not from Thucydides. But from this extreme statement there seems to be reason for dissent. Would Epicurus, who was himself an Athenian resident, living but a hundred years after Thucydides, misunderstand the historian as Lucretius gives evidence of doing? A comparison of Thucydides II, 47–54 with Lucretius VI, 1138–1286, will show several instances in which the poet has either wilfully or ignorantly misrepresented his model. For example observe the difference between this declaration of Thucydides—τῶν γε ἀκρωτηρίων ἀντίληψις αὐτοῦ ἐπεσήμαινε· κατέσκηπτε γὰρ ἐς αἰδοῖα καὶ ἐς ἄκρας χεῖρας καὶ πόδας, καὶ πολλοὶ στερισκόμενοι τούτων διέφυγον, εἰσὶ δ' οἳ καὶ τῶν ὀφθαλμῶν[2]—and the verses of Lucretius on the same matter :

. . . *tamen in nervos huic morbus et artus*
Ibat et in partis genitalis corporis ipsas.
Et graviter partim metuentes limina leti
Vivebant ferro privati parte virili,
Et manibus sine nonnulli pedibusque manebant
In vita tamen et perdebant lumina partim:
Usque adeo mortis mortus his incesserat acer.[3]

In view of the intense desire of Lucretius to turn to account every opportunity to point a moral, is it not possible that he purposely

---

[1] Compare the statements of Epicurus recorded by Diogenes Laertius, X, 91-115, with Lucretius VI. Cf. E. G. Sihler, *Transactions Am. Phil. Ass.*, 1898.
[2] *D. Bello Peloponnesiaco.* II. 49. 7. 8. Cf. Munro. II. pp. 391-401.
[3] VI. 1206 12.

perverted this passage from Thucydides in order to reinforce his position? The misery of the plague-stricken victims was such that suicide would seem to be reasonable and desirable; but fear of death—that ever-present terror of men's lives—withheld them from this and induced them to deprive themselves of certain diseased members that life might be prolonged.

There is another extreme view regarding the question under discussion, which is represented by those scholars who maintain that Lucretius was a man of great independent research. These men light uncritically upon any point of doctrinal identity, particularly in Book VI, and forthwith are eager to ascribe original investigation to Lucretius.[1] There can be no doubt also that "he was endowed not only with the poet's susceptibility to the movement and beauty of the outside world, but also with the observing faculty and curiosity of a naturalist;"[2] but it must be ever kept in mind that distinctive Epicureanism does not consist of the study of the minutiae of physical facts for the purpose of presenting a well articulated system of natural philosophy, but is practically the metaphysical employment of observed phenomena to demonstrate the folly of fearing the gods or death. It is necessary always to differentiate the γνήσιος φυσιολογία of Epicurus, which is substantially given in Books I to earlier parts of V, from the specific elucidation of physical phenomena in Book VI, which agrees, so far as these are concerned, with the letter to Pythocles.[3] Unquestionably in the field of physical research Lucretius does evince some traces of independent investigation. But there is little if any evidence that in what may be called the true Epicureanism he is similarly self-reliant.

As to the general question of originality of treatment, it is clear that a middle ground between the extreme positions herein illustrated must be adopted. Some personal study of Empedocles, as will be

---

[1] *Vide* Paulus Rusch : *De Posidonio Lucreti Cari Auctore in Carmine De Rerum Natura VI.*, Greifswald, 1882 [a doctor's dissertation], who tries to trace points in Book VI even to Posidonius. Rusch is evidently aware of his oddity, for on p. 51 he says : *Valde temerarius fortasse visus sum, quod temptavi carminis poetae Romani, quem strenuum Epicureum fuisse viri docti persuasum habebant vel etiam Stoicum auctorem monstrare.*
[2] Sellar, *Roman Poets of the Republic*, p. 292.
[3] *Diog. Laer..* X. 84. *sqq.*

seen hereafter, must be accredited to Lucretius. And doubtless other philosophers, such as Democritus, Anaxagoras, Heraclitus, and even Plato, were investigated by the poet for himself.[1] Still it must always remain true that the chief service which Lucretius rendered to philosophy was the presentation in an attractive form of the teachings of Epicurus, who, to judge from his literary remains, was utterly incapable of producing an exposition of his creed so admirable in every way as that contained in the *De Rerum Natura*.[2] Lucretius perhaps added nothing of importance to the Epicurean system, but he imparted a wondrous vitality and buoyancy to its heavy, mechanical doctrines.

An emphatic variation is observable in the position which Lucretius assumes towards the leaders of the several schools of philosophy which he criticises. The bulk of his discussion touching these schemes of thought is found in Book I, though marks of controversy are discoverable throughout the entire poem. In these polemical passages Lucretius occasionally exhibits a spirit alike friendly and appreciative towards the champions of faiths hostile to his own, though more frequently he inveighs bitterly against those whose doctrines oppose the tenets of Epicurus. In this disposition to treat fairly his antagonists, the disciple excelled the teacher; for Epicurus had apparently become so blinded by personal vanity, and so intoxicated by the idolatry of his followers, as to be no longer able to discern any feature of excellence outside his own narrow circle of speculation. Lucretius, on the other hand, shows a commendable desire to give honor to whom honor is due. It will perhaps facilitate our discussion of the controversial elements in Lucretius if we consider first those points of contact between the poet and the subjects of his criticism which reveal a sentiment of friendliness, and secondly those which betray an unmistakable attitude of hostility.

---

[1] Munro, II, p. 9.
[2] Masson, *Atomic Theory of Lucretius*, p. 4.

I.

PHILOSOPHERS WITH WHOM LUCRETIUS CONTENDS AMICABLY.

In placing his discussion of the Pre-Socratic Physicists in the very fore-front of his poem Lucretius has shown a distinctive trait of his school, which is also amply illustrated in the *Volumina Herculanensia;* for Epicurean teachers were evidently in the habit of commencing an exposition of their own doctrines by making a criticism upon other systems of natural philosophy.[1] But mere conformity to a traditional method is not a sufficient explanation of the poet's introduction of controversy at such an early stage in the development of his theme. There was an immediate occasion to justify the procedure. Lucretius has sometimes been accused of being too belligerent, of forcing a conflict when the reasons for warfare were somewhat obscure.[2] Perhaps he does sometimes bristle with steel when no enemy is visible, but surely this complaint cannot be lodged against him with propriety in this instance. For the long polemical section beginning at I, 635, appears to arise out of the very necessities of Lucretius' argument. It must be remembered that his chief aim is to cleanse human life and deliver the soul of man from the terrors of superstition, which he believes are engendered by ignorance of the constitution of nature, of the origin of the material universe and of the causes of natural phenomena. These mental disturbances are only to be conquered by letting in the light of reason upon the processes of nature.

> *Hunc igitur terrorem animi tenebrasque necessest*
> *Non radii solis neque lucida tela diei*
> *Discutiant, sed naturae species ratioque—*[3]

is the burden of the refrain he loves to repeat But in order to establish knowledge, it is first necessary to make inquiry into the

---

[1] Stickney, *De Natura Deorum*, p. 23.
[2] Sellar, *Roman Poets of the Republic*, p. 298.
[3] I, 146-8 ; II. 59-61 ; III, 91-3 ; VI, 39-41.

primary principles of being. Now from the earliest times the effort of all framers of ontological systems has been to discover the original substance or substances from which all existing things have come into being. And a great variety of results have been reached by the investigations of primitive philosophers. Lucretius discards the findings of all these researchers except Democritus, and cordially following Epicurus in this regard, adopts the atomistic theory, which is attributed to Leucippus and Democritus jointly, and declares that the original substances are atoms and the void—ἄτομα καὶ κενόν—*materies et inane*. He then proceeds to lay down and demonstrate his propositions relative to the constitution of matter. He enunciates the two great laws of nature :

Nullam rem e nilo gigni divinitus unquam.[1]

*. . . In sua corpora rursum
Dissoluat natura neque ad nilum interemat res.*[2]

He expounds the nature of the atoms, and asserts their eternity, solidity, indivisibility, and then pauses to enter upon a controversy with those philosophers whose theories are utterly irreconcilable with his own. This appears to be unavoidable with a man of his earnestness. He evidently feels that until these false teachings have been neutralized he cannot proceed with his constructive argument.

However he does not treat all of these notable predecessors with unmitigated severity. Indeed in some instances his considerateness amounts to praise :

*Quamquam multa bene ac divinitus invenientes
Ex adyto tamquam cordis responsa dedere
Sanctius et multo certa ratione magis quam
Pythia quae tripode a Phoebi lauroque profatur,
Principiis tamen in rerum fecere ruinas
Et graviter magni magno cecidere ibi casu.*[3]

But he is emphatic in denunciation of their theories. He breaks with all the early Ionic and Eleatic philosophers, Thales, Anaximenes,

---

[1] I, 150.
[2] I, 215, 16.
[3] I, 736-41.

Pherecydes, Xenophanes, Parmenides and the rest, who call any one or more substances original matter. The names of these thinkers are not mentioned by Lucretius, but he distinctly condemns their physical doctrines.

*Quapropter qui materiem rerum esse putarunt
Ignem atque ex igni summam consistere posse,
Et qui principium gignundis aera rebus
Constituere, aut umorem quicumque putarunt
Fingere res ipsum per se, terramve creare
Omnia et in rerum naturas vertier omnis,
Magno opere a vero longe derrasse videntur.
Adde etiam qui conduplicant primordia rerum
Aera iungentes igni terramque liquori,
Et qui quattuor ex rebus posse omnia rentur
Ex igni terra atque anima procrescere et imbri.*[1]

1. EMPEDOCLES.

The occasion of Lucretius' attack upon Empedocles, if it can properly be denominated such, is the position which he occupies among those physicists who have named one or more substances as primordial matter. Were it not for this we may well conjecture that Lucretius would have paid an honest tribute of respect and obligation to this illustrious sage and passed on to other subjects of criticism. But he regards Empedocles as the most dominant figure among those philosophers who make a combination of certain substances their original matter.[2] And in this he is unquestionably correct. Aristotle bears witness to the fact that Empedocles first declared that there were four elements, to which Plato subsequently gave the designation στοιχεῖα.[3]

Ἐδόκει δὲ αὐτῷ τάδε· Στοιχεῖα μὲν εἶναι τέτταρα, πῦρ, ὕδωρ, γῆν, ἀέρα· φιλίαν τε ᾗ συγκρίνεται, καὶ νεῖκος ᾧ διακρίνεται. Φησὶ δ' οὕτω,

Ζεὺς ἀργὴς, Ἥρη τε φερέσβιος, ἠδ' Ἀϊδωνεὺς,
Νῆστίς θ', ἣ δακρύοις ἐπιπικροῖ ὄμμα βρότειον.

---
[1] I, 705-15.
[2] *Quorum Acragantinus cum primis Empedocles est.* I. 716.
[3] Ritter et Preller, *Hist. Phil. Graec.*, 131, a.

Δία μὲν, τὸ πῦρ λέγων· Ἥρην δὲ, τὴν γῆν· Ἀϊδωνέα δε, τὸν ἀέρα· Νῆστιν δὲ, τὸ ὕδωρ·¹

Holding such principles Empedocles would inevitably fall under the censure of Lucretius. Yet his position is exceptional. He is the only philosopher among those from whom the poet differs, with whose name laudation is coupled. But warm and enthusiastic is the eulogium of Lucretius upon him. He is the chief glory of the wonderful three-cornered Sicilian isle, —

> *Quae cum magna modis multis miranda videtur*
> *Gentibus humanis regio visendaque fertur,*
> *Rebus opima bonis, multa munita virum vi,*
> *Nil tamen hoc habuisse viro praeclarius in se*
> *Nec sanctum magis et mirum carumque videtur.*
> *Carmina quin etiam divini pectoris eius*
> *Vociferantur et exponunt praeclara reperta.*
> *Ut vix humana videatur stirpe creatus.*²

But more significant than any verbal praise which Lucretius bestows upon Empedocles is the internal evidence which his poem discloses of his affectionate study of the philosopher, and his copious use of the style of utterance and philosophical conceptions of Empedocles, notwithstanding the general disagreement between their doctrines. Lucretius was greatly indebted to Empedocles in various ways. He doubtless regarded the περὶ φύσεως of the latter as in some sense his poetic model.³ The genius of Empedocles was celebrated by Aristotle, and may well have influenced the character of Lucretius' composition. Ἐν δὲ τῷ περὶ ποιητῶν φησιν, ὅτι καὶ Ὁμηρικὸς ὁ Ἐμπεδοκλῆς, καὶ δεινὸς περὶ τὴν φράσιν γέγονε, μεταφορικός τε ὤν, καὶ τοῖς ἄλλοις τοῖς περὶ ποιητικὴν ἐπιτεύγμασι χρώμενος.⁴ In view of the fact that critics have been able to designate verses in both authors which bear a distinct Homeric⁵ flavor, we may infer, perhaps, that the influence of Empedocles upon Lucretius was even more subtle than the latter

---

¹*Diog. Laer.*, VIII, 76.
² I, 726–33.
³ Munro, II, p. 90. Cf. *Ib.*, p. 32.
⁴ *Diog. Laer.*, VIII, 57.
⁵ Sellar, *Roman Poets of the Republic*, p. 302.

was himself aware. But the traces of a more direct influence are abundant. The first fundamental principle, which Lucretius establishes at the outset of his argument, is that nothing can be created from nothing by divine agency ; and the second is like unto it, that nothing already in existence can ever be annihilated. But the very content and form of these propositions reflect the doctrine of Empedocles.

Nullam rem e nilo gigni divinitus unquam,

was evidently suggested by the lines of the older poem περὶ φύσεως :

ἐκ τοῦ γὰρ μὴ ἐόντος ἀμήχανόν ἐστι γενέσθαι
τό τ' ἐὸν ἐξόλλυσθαι ἀνήνυστον καὶ ἄπρηκτον.[1]

What has the appearance of generation and decay in the view of Empedocles is in reality but combination and separation. And with this view Lucretius agrees perfectly, the arguments which he addresses in defense of his theory being both interesting and pertinent.[2] We are indebted to Aemilius Hallier[3] for an exhaustive presentation of the evidences of Lucretius' familiarity with Empedocles. This painstaking writer has collated a considerable body of passages from the two poets which amply justify the opinion that the *De Rerum Natura* owes much to the περὶ φύσεως, both in literary style and in philosophic material. There exists, for example, a similarity of grammatical and rhetorical forms in these productions which is worthy of remark. Both poets are also given to an almost excessive use of iteration, Lucretius in particular being prone to this habit. Again, both freely employ tmesis, another indication, perhaps, of the influence of the Homeric verse upon Empedocles who studied it. Then, too, there are palpable imitations of the elder poet in the phraseology of Lucretius. Compare the following lines :

αὐτὰρ ἐγὼ παλίνορσος ἐλεύσομαι ἐς πόρον ὕμνων.[4]
Sed nunc ut repetam coeptum pertexere dictis.[5]

---

[1] *Emped.*, 48, 49, Sellar, *Roman Poets of the Republic*, p. 300.
[2] I, 159-328.
[3] *Lucreti Carmina e Fragmentis Empedoclis Adumbrata*, Jena, 1857, (A doctor's dissertation).
[4] *Emped.*, 169, Hallier. p. 13.
[5] *Lucret.*, I, 418.

γίγνοντ' ἄνθρωποί τε καὶ ἄλλων ἔθνεα θηρῶν.[1]
Et genus humanum, parit omnia saecla ferarum.[2]

Again, there are instances of the employment of identical similes by both poets:

. . . γῆς ἱδρῶτα θάλασσαν.[3]

. *expressus salsus de corpore sudor.*[4]

Munro[5] has pointed out that the lines—

Nec tamen hanc possis oculorum subdere visu
Nec iacere indu manus, via qua munita fidei
Proxima fert humanum in pectus templaque mentis—[6]

are translated from this passage of Empedocles:

οὐκ ἔστιν πελάσασθ' οὐδ' ὀφθαλμοῖσιν ἐφικτὸν
ἡμετέροις ἢ χερσὶ λαβεῖν ᾗπερ γε μεγίστη
πειθοῦς ἀνθρώποισιν ἁμαξιτὸς εἰς φρένα πίπτει.[7]

But the marks of doctrinal agreement in the works of these poet-philosophers are even more significant than resemblances of composition. While Empedocles and Lucretius differ on many of the questions involved in their several discussions of the nature of things, there are not a few notable points of coincidence in their writings. They are of one mind touching the eternity of matter:

φύσις οὐδενός ἐστιν ἁπάντων
θνητῶν, οὐδέ τις οὐλομένου θανάτοιο τελευτή,
. . . φύσις δ' ἐπὶ τοῖς ὀνομάζεται ἀνθρώποισιν.[8]

Quod si in eo spatio atque anteacta aetate fuere
E quibus haec rerum consistit summa refecta,
Immortali sunt natura praedita certe,
Haut igitur possunt ad nilum quaeque reverti.

---

[1] *Emped.*, 115, Hallier, p. 13.
[2] *Lucret.*, II, 995.
[3] *Emped.*, 165.
[4] *Lucret.*, V, 487.
[5] II, 290.
[6] *Lucret.*, V, 101-3.
[7] *Emped.*, 356.
[8] *Ib.*, 36, 37, 39, Hallier, p. 15.

*Denique res omnis eadem vis causaque volgo
Conficeret, nisi materies aeterna teneret,
Inter se nexu minus aut magis indupedita.*[1]

Cognate with this doctrine is the theory of the constancy of the sum of matter in the universe, on which they are agreed:

οὐδέ τι τοῦ παντὸς κενεὸν πέλει οὐδὲ περισσόν.
τοῦτο δ' ἐπαυξήσειε τὸ πᾶν τί κε καὶ πόθεν ἐλθόν;
πῆ δέ κε καὶ ἀπολοίατ'; ἐπεὶ τῶνδ' οὐδὲν ἔρημον.
ἀλλ' αὔτ' ἔστιν ταῦτα.[2]

Nam neque adaugescit quicquam neque deperit inde.

. . . .

*Nec rerum summam commutare ulla potest vis;
Nam neque quo possit genus ullum materiai
Effugere ex omni, quicquam est extra, neque in omne
Unde coorta queat nova vis inrumpere et omnem
Naturam rerum mutare et vertere motus.*[3]

There is reason to suppose that the doctrine that the soul is blood, to which Lucretius[4] refers, is derived from Empedocles, who says:

αἷμα γὰρ ἀνθρώποις περικάρδιόν ἐστι νόημα.[5]

They are in accord also on the doctrine that all things came into existence by the conjunction or combination of the eternal and infinitesimal *semina*.

ἀλλὰ μόνον μίξις τε διάλλαξίς τε μιγέντων
ἐστί.[6]

. . . *certa suo quia tempore semina rerum
Cum confluxerunt, patefit quodcumque creatur.*[7]

In their explanations of the phenomena of nature there are likewise important resemblances in Empedocles and Lucretius. The eclipse of the sun affords this parallel:

---

[1] *Lucret.*, I, 234-40.
[2] *Emped.* 91-94. Hallier, p. 16.
[3] *Lucret.*, II, 296, 303-307.
[4] III. 43.
[5] *Emped.*, 317. Munro, II, p. 179.
[6] *Emped.*, 38, 39. Hallier, p. 22.
[7] *Lucret.*, I, 176, 177.

ἐπεσκίασεν δέ οἱ αὐγὰς
ἰσταμένη καθύπερθεν, ἐπεσκνίφωσε δὲ γαίης,
τόσσον ὅσον τ' εὖρος γλαυκώπιδος ἔπλετο μήνης.[1]

Nam cur luna queat terram secludere solis
Lumine et a terris altum caput obstruere ei,
Obiciens caecum radiis ardentibus orbem.[2]

The growth of plants and trees is explained in a similar fashion by each :

Ἐμπεδοκλῆς πρῶτα τὰ δένδρα τῶν ζῴων ἐκ γῆς ἀναδῦναι φησι, πρὶν τὸν ἥλιον περιαπλωθῆναι καὶ πρὶν ἡμέραν καὶ νύκτα διακριθῆναι· διὰ δὲ συμμετρίαν τῆς κράσεως τὸν τοῦ ἄρρενος καὶ τοῦ θήλεος περιέχειν λόγον· αὔξεσθαι δὲ ὑπὸ τοῦ ἐν τῇ γῇ θερμοῦ διαιρόμενα, ὥστε γῆς εἶναι μέρη, καθάπερ καὶ τὰ ἔμβρυα τὰ ἐν τῇ γαστρὶ τῆς μήτρας μέρη.[3]

Principio genus herbarum viridemque nitorem
Terra dedit circum collis camposque per omnis,
Florida fulserunt viridanti prata colore,
Arborisque datumst variis exinde per auras
Crescendi magnum inmissis certamen habenis.
Ut pluma atque pili primum saetaeque creantur
Quadripedum membris et corpore pennipotentum,
Sic nova tum tellus herbas virgultaque primum
Sustulit, inde loci mortalia saecla creavit
Multa modis multis varia ratione coorta.[4]

Lightning is explained by both as the result of fire submerged in clouds :

καίτοι τινὲς λέγουσιν ὡς ἐν τοῖς νέφεσιν ἐγγίνεται πῦρ· τοῦτο δ' Ἐμπεδοκλῆς μέν φησιν εἶναι τὸ ἐμπεριλαμβανόμενον τῶν τοῦ ἡλίου ἀκτίνων.[5]

Hac etiam fit uti de causa mobilis ille
Devolet in terram liquidi calor aureus ignis,
Semina quod nubes ipsas permulta necessust
Ignis habere; etenim cum sunt umore sine ullo,
Flammeus est plerumque colos et splendidus ollis.

---

[1] *Emped.*, 157–9, Hallier, p. 31.
[2] *Lucret.*, V, 753–5.
[3] *Plac.*, V, 26. 4 *Dox.*, 438, Ritter et Preller, 136.
[4] *Lucret.*, V, 783–92.
[5] *Aristotle, Meteor,* II, 9, p. 369. B. 11. quoted by Hallier, p. 35.

EMPEDOCLES.   27

Quin etiam solis de lumine multa necesses
Concipere, ut merito rubeant ignesque profundant.[1]

Epicurus doubtless borrowed his notion of effluxes[2] (ἀπόρροιαι) from Empedocles to explain the phenomena of perception. σκόπει δὴ κατ' Ἐμπεδοκλέα γνοὺς ὅτι πάντων εἰσὶν ἀπορροαὶ ὅσσ' ἐγένοντο· οὐ γὰρ ζῴων μόνον οὐδὲ φυτῶν, οὐδὲ γῆς καὶ θαλάττης, ἀλλὰ καὶ λίθων ἄπεισιν ἐνδελεχῶς πολλὰ ῥεύματα καὶ λίθων καὶ σιδήρου.[3] These emanations he termed εἴδωλα, and Lucretius has adopted the same method of accounting for sense perceptions, devoting a large proportion of Book IV to the consideration of what he denominates *simulacra*. Sellar[4] has called attention to the fact that the principle of beauty and life in the universe figures in the verses of both writers under the symbol of the goddess of love—Empedocles employing the form Κύπρι Βασίλεια; Lucretius, *alma Venus, genetrix*. Zeller draws an interesting parallel between the primitive substances of Empedocles (which are subject to no qualitative changes, and combine only through the entrance of the particles of one body into the intervals between the parts of another) and the Atoms and Void of the Democritean system.[5] Perhaps a similar comparison between the Empedoclean doctrine of Love and Hate and the atomistic theory of the eternal conflict and conjunction would be equally justifiable. τὰ μὲν σωματικὰ στοιχεῖα ποιεῖ τέτταρα, πῦρ καὶ ἀέρα καὶ ὕδωρ καὶ γῆν, ἀΐδια μὲν ὄντα πλήθει καὶ ὀλιγότητι, μεταβάλλοντα δὲ κατὰ τὴν σύγκρισιν καὶ διάκρισιν, τὰς δὲ κυρίως ἀρχάς, ὑφ' ὧν κινεῖται ταῦτα, φιλίαν καὶ νεῖκος. δεῖ γὰρ διατελεῖν ἐναλλὰξ κινούμενα τὰ στοιχεῖα, ποτὲ μὲν ὑπὸ τῆς φιλίας συγκρινόμενα, ποτὲ δὲ ὑπὸ τοῦ νείκους διακρινόμενα.[6] Compare this statement with the lines of Lucretius—

---

[1] *Lucret.*, VI, 204-210.
[2] *Diog. Laert.*, X, 46-53.
[3] *Plutarch, Qu. Nat.*, 19, 3, in Ritter et Preller, 132 h. Cf. Zeller, *Pre-Socratic Philosophy*, II, p. 165.
[4] *Roman Poets of the Republic*, p. 300. Cf. Hallier, p. 25.
[5] "This whole theory is closely allied to that of the Atomists. The small, invisible particles take the place of the atoms, and pores the place of void. The Atomists see in bodies a mass of atoms separated by empty interspaces; Empedocles sees in them a mass of particles which have certain openings between them, etc.," Zeller, *Pre-Socratic Philosophy*, II, p. 135. Cf. Munro, II, p. 92.
[6] *Simpl. Phys.*, 6 v., 25, 21. D., in Ritter et Preller, 132 h.

*Nec sic interemit mors res ut materiai
Corpora conficiat, sed coetum dissupat ollis
Inde aliis aliud coniungit.*[1]

Is there not at least some external resemblance between these declarations of the method by which the forces of nature operate? The comparisons thus far instituted by no means exhaust the possibilities of the subject, but are sufficient to demonstrate the intimate acquaintance of Lucretius with Empedocles, and his indisputable obligation to the older poet. The eulogy which he pronounces upon Empedocles is not merely the praise of an admirer; it is an expression of gratitude from a beneficiary.

But despite his honorable acknowledgment of the greatness of Empedocles, Lucretius is bound in all sincerity to combat certain of his physicial doctrines and deductions as wholly inconsistent with a true philosophy of the universe. Perhaps it would be more just to say that in his strictures upon Empedocles Lucretius is aiming at the whole school of philosophers who name any qualitative substance or substances as primal matter, rather than at a single teacher. These, in his judgment, which he presents with considerable fullness, have all gone astray with regard to *primordia*. And the arguments adduced against one are also valid against all. Yet it is possible in a few instances to distinguish the shafts which are especially directed toward Empedocles.

Lucretius, in the first place, condemns the Agrigentine philosopher for denying void, while at the same time he admits motions to things.

*Primum quod motus exempto rebus inani
Constituunt, et res mollis rarasque relinquont,
Aera solem ignem terras animalia frugis,
Nec tamen admiscent in eorum corpus inane.*[2]

The testimony of Aristotle is clear on this point: ἔνιοι μὲν οὖν τῶν μὴ φασκόντων εἶναι κενὸν οὐδὲν διώρισαν περὶ κούφου καὶ βαρέος οἷον 'Αναξαγόρας καὶ 'Εμπεδοκλῆς.[3] But Empedocles is himself equally plain:

---

[1] II. 1002-4. Cf. II. 569-80.
[2] I. 742-45.
[3] *De Caelo.* IV. 2, 309. a 19. Ritter et Preller, 132 f.

οὐδέ τι τοῦ παντὸς κενεὸν πέλει οὐδὲ περισσόν.¹

This position Lucretius rightfully regards as incongruous. Indeed, as already indicated, the Empedoclean doctrine of primitive substances and their method of combination leads logically and almost inevitably to something very much akin to the atomistic hypothesis. For atoms minute particles of matter are substituted, and for void we have pores or interstices Combination is effected according to a certain elective affinity, like particles being attracted by like and dissimilar particles being mutually repellent. Notwithstanding the palpable resemblances thus exhibited, Empedocles rejects the fundamental principles of the atomists, an inconsistency which Aristotle was quick to discover.

σχεδὸν δὲ καὶ Ἐμπεδοκλεῖ ἀναγκαῖον λέγειν, ὥσπερ καὶ Λεύκιππός φησιν. εἶναι γὰρ ἄττα στερεά, ἀδιαίρετα δέ, εἰ μὴ πάντη πόροι συνεχεῖς εἰσιν.²

Lucretius furthermore exposes the fallacy of assigning softness to *primordia* and still supposing them immortal.

Huc accedit item, quoniam primordia rerum
Mollia constituunt, quae nos nativa videmus
Esse et mortali cum corpore funditus, utqui
Debeat ad nilum iam rerum summa reverti
*De niloque renata vigescere copia rerum.*³

This disastrous conclusion Empedocles distinctly disavows:

φύσις οὐδενός ἐστιν ἁπάντων
θνητῶν, οὐδέ τις οὐλομένου θανάτοιο τελευτή.
ἐκ τε γὰρ οὐδάμ' ἐόντος ἀμήχανόν ἐστι γενέσθαι,
καί τ' ἐὸν ἐξαπολέσθαι ἀνήνυστον καὶ ἄπυστον.
αἶψα δὲ θνήτ' ἐφύοντο τὰ πρὶν μάθον ἀθάνατ' εἶναι.⁴

Lucretius next shows the inconsistency of maintaining that all things are made out of four elements and reduced to them again, inasmuch as in this way the things are the *primordia* of the elements quite as truly as the elements are of the things.

---
[1] *Emped.*, 91, in Fairbanks' *First Philosophers of Greece*, p. 168.
[2] Aristotle. *Gen. et Corr.*, I, 1, 325 *b*, 5. in Zeller, *Pre-Socratic Philosophy*, II, p. 136. 2.
[3] I. 753-57.
[4] *Emped.*, 77. 78, 81, 82. 178. Fairbanks, pp. 162, 164, 180. Munro, II, p. 93.

*Denique quattuor ex rebus si cuncta creantur
Atque in eas rursum res omnia dissoluuntur,
Qui magis illa queunt rerum primordia dici
Quam contra res illorum retroque putari?
Alternis gignuntur enim mutantque colorem
Et totam inter se naturam tempore ab omni.*[1]

Lucretius also contends more pointedly against the Heracliteans, perhaps, than against Empedocles, though the latter must be partially intended,[2] that the supposed process from fire to air, water, earth, and thence in reverse order, involves the theory that the *primordia* must be distinct from these elements and unchangeable, otherwise all things would ultimately be annihilated.[3]

Lucretius and Empedocles took opposite positions with reference to the value of the perceptions as media of knowledge. The former declared the senses to be infallible guides to truth.

*Non modo enim ratio ruat omnis, vita quoque ipsa
Concidat extemplo, nisi credere sensibus ausis.*[4]

The latter asserted that the senses are wholly unreliable, and enjoined men to acquire knowledge of the nature of things by reflection.

ἀλλ' ἄγ' ἄθρει πάσῃ παλάμῃ πῇ δῆλον ἕκαστον,
μήτε τιν' ὄψιν ἔχων πίστει πλέον ἢ κατ' ἀκουὴν
μήτ' ἀκοὴν ἐρίδουπον ὑπὲρ τρανώματα γλώσσης
μήτε τι τῶν ἄλλων, ὁπόσων πόρος ἐστὶ νοῆσαι,
γυίων πίστιν ἔρυκε, νόει δ' ᾗ δῆλον ἕκαστον.[5]

Lucretius maintains that the soul perishes with the body and employs much labor and ingenuity to make good his argument.[6] But Empedocles taught the doctrine of a future life and the transmigration of spirits.

---

[1] I, 763-68.
[2] Hallier, p. 20, insists that Lucretius refers in this passage to Heraclitus alone, but Munro, II, p. 95, says Empedocles was also included.
[3] I, 782-802.
[4] IV, 507-8.
[5] *Emped.*, 19-23, in Fairbanks' *First Philosophers of Greece*, p. 160.
[6] III, 417-829.

ἤδη γάρ ποτ' ἐγὼ γενόμην κοῦρός τε κόρη τε
θάμνος τ' οἰωνός τε καὶ εἰν ἅλι ἔλλοπος ἰχθύς.[1]

Lucretius agrees with Empedocles in the theory that Nature tried many experiments and constructed many malformations, which were doomed to destruction, before she hit upon perfection in the various species.

πολλὰ μὲν ἀμφιπρόσωπα καὶ ἀμφίστερν' ἐφύοντο,
. . . μεμιγμένα τῇ μὲν ἀπ' ἀνδρῶν,
τῇ δὲ γυναικοφυῆ, στείροις ἠσκημένα γυίοις.[2]

With this declaration of Empedocles may be compared a passage from Lucretius too lengthy for quotation in this place, but equally explicit on the same theory.[3] But Lucretius condemns centaurs and other beings of a two-fold nature as impossible,[4] though Empedocles does not hesitate to affirm his credence in them:

βουγενῆ ἀνδρόπρωρα, τὰ δ' ἔμπαλιν ἐξανέτελλον
ἀνδροφυῆ βούκρανα.[5]

Lucretius likewise dissents entirely from the doctrine that primary bodies worked teleologically, an idea which Empedocles embraces with enthusiasm, and the promulgation of which constitutes him according to Zeller "the earliest precursor of Darwin."[6]

ᾗ πολλαὶ μὲν κόρσαι ἀναύχενες ἐβλάστησαν,
γυμνοὶ δ' ἐπλάζοντο βραχίονες εὔνιδες ὤμων,
ὄμματα δ' οἶ' ἐπλανᾶτο πενητεύοντα μετώπων.

But Love—Ἀφροδίτη—fashioned these together into comely and appropriate unions.

αὐτὰρ ἐπεὶ κατὰ μεῖζον ἐμίσγετο δαίμονι δαίμων,
ταῦτά τε συμπίπτεσκον ὅπη συνέκυρσεν ἕκαστα,
ἄλλα τε πρὸς τοῖς πολλὰ διηνεκῆ ἐξεγένοντο.[7]

---

[1] *Emped.*, 384, 85. Fairbanks, p. 206. *Diog. Laer.*, VIII, 76.
[2] *Emped.*, 257, 259, 260. Fairbanks, p. 190.
[3] V, 837-54.
[4] IV, 878-924. Cf. Munro, II, pp. 328-9.
[5] *Emped.*, 258, 59. Fairbanks, p. 190.
[6] *Pre-Socratic Philosophy*, II, p. 206.
[7] *Emped.*, 244-46, 254-56. Fairbanks, pp. 188-90. Cf. Munro, II, p. 326.

So Empedocles expresses himself, while Lucretius vehemently denounces the doctrine of final causes in a passage [1] which is directed, as we shall see hereafter, primarily against the Stoics. Faculties and functions were not created for predestined ends, but finding himself possessed of powers and appliances man uses them for his advantage.

*Nil ideo quoniam natumst in corpore ut uti
Possemus, sed quod natumst id procreat usum.*[2]

It was the habit of the Epicurean school to include Empedocles in the catalogue of philosophers to be derided and condemned, as Cicero and Plutarch testify,[3] but Lucretius commends the author as much as he combats him, and discloses in his lines an indebtedness to Empedocles which he is not averse from paying.

2. ANAXAGORAS.

*Nunc et Anaxagorae scrutemur homoeomerian
Quam Grai memorant nec nostra dicere lingua
Concedit nobis patrii sermonis egestas,
Sed tamen ipsam rem facilest exponere verbis.*[4]

With these words Lucretius introduces a philosopher for whom he has a degree of personal esteem, and with whom the Epicurean school had some natural affiliation. The opinion which Epicurus held concerning Anaxagoras was singularly high.

Μάλιστα δ' ἀπεδέχετο, φησὶ Διοκλῆς, τῶν ἀρχαίων Ἀναξαγόραν, καίτοι ἔν τισιν ἀντειρηκὼς αὐτῷ.[5]

In addition to this evidence of his warm regard Epicurus, it has been conjectured, furnishes further proof in the freedom with which in his letter to Pythocles he employs the views of

---
[1] IV, 823-57.
[2] IV, 834-5.
[3] Usener, *Epicurea*, pp. 175. 10 ; 187, 19.
[4] I, 830-32.
[5] *Diog. Laer.*, X, 12.

Anaxagoras in setting forth a variety of explanations for remarkable physical phenomena. A comparison of the extant fragments of Anaxagoras and the records of his opinions in other writings with certain statements of Epicurus in the document referred to has led to this conviction. Attention has been especially directed by Usener [1] to the causes assigned for the rising and setting of the sun, moon and stars; the intertropical movement of the sun and moon; the successive phases of the moon; the apparition of a face in the orb of the moon; the eclipses of the sun and moon; and the phenomena of lightning, earthquakes and hail.[2]

Moreover there is a general sense in which Anaxagoras occupies a common ground with Empedocles, Leucippus and Democritus.[3] On the proposition of Parmenides that generation and destruction in the ordinary meaning of those terms are impossible Anaxagoras is in agreement with the Atomists and the Epicureans. With them also he proceeds upon the supposition that there are certain original and immutable substances, out of which were evolved all things by combination and separation in space. There is this fundamental difference, however, between Anaxagoras and the contemporaneous philosophers with whom he contended: The latter conceived primitive matter without the qualities of things in being. Empedocles names four elements distinct in quality. Democritus designates atoms unlimited in form and multitude and alike in quality as primordial matter. Anaxagoras, on the other hand, regards original and elementary substances as possessing all the qualities and differences of things derived, and conceives them infinite in number and kind, a theory which creates a radical divergence between himself and the Atomists.

There is another position which separates Anaxagoras from the systems named. They explain motion, which is the cause of all combination, separation and order in the universe, by forces inherent in matter; Empedocles by the mythical contrivance of Love and Hate, the Atomists by the force of gravity. But Anaxagoras asserts that motion must be attributed to the operation of immaterial

---

[1] *Epicurea.* p. 400.
[2] *Diog. Laer.*, X. 92-96. 101. 105. 106.
[3] Zeller, *Pre-Socratic Philosophy.* II. p. 330.

energy, and places Mind—νοῦς—in opposition to matter as the origin of motion and order.

In support of the statement that Anaxagoras, like Epicurus, regarded generation and destruction as in reality only combination (σύγκρισις) and separation (διάκρισις), we have the affirmation of the philosopher himself:

τὸ δὲ γίνεσθαι καὶ ἀπόλλυσθαι οὐκ ὀρθῶς νομίζουσιν οἱ Ἕλληνες· οὐδὲν γὰρ χρῆμα γίνεται οὐδὲ ἀπόλλυται, ἀλλ᾽ ἀπὸ ἐόντων χρημάτων συμμίσγεταί τε καὶ διακρίνεται. καὶ οὕτως ἂν ὀρθῶς καλοῖεν τό τε γίνεσθαι συμμίσγεσθαι καὶ τὸ ἀπόλλυσθαι διακρίνεσθαι.[1]

On this passage Zeller makes the following comment—"The treatise of Anaxagoras did not begin with these words ; but that is, of course, no reason why they should not form the starting-point of his system."[2] It has already been shown how fundamental this doctrine is to the Epicurean philosophy. Indeed Munro calls this fragment of Anaxagoras "an aphorism which Epicurus might have wholly adopted.[3] Aristotle has preserved the following—

ἔοικε δὲ Ἀναξαγόρας ἄπειρα οὕτως οἰηθῆναι διὰ τὸ ὑπολαμβάνειν τὴν κοινὴν δόξαν τῶν φυσικῶν εἶναι ἀληθῆ, ὡς οὐ γινομένου οὐδενὸς ἐκ τοῦ μὴ ὄντος· διὰ τοῦτο γὰρ οὕτω λέγουσιν, ἦν ὁμοῦ τὰ πάντα, καὶ τὸ γίνεσθαι τοιόνδε καθέστηκεν ἀλλοιοῦσθαι.[4]

In this connection we may also quote :

ὡς καὶ Ἀναξαγόρας καὶ Εὐριπίδης·
θνῄσκει δ᾽ οὐδὲν τῶν γιγνομένων
διακρινόμενον δ᾽ ἄλλο πρὸς ἄλλο
μορφὰς ἑτέρας ἀπέδειξεν.[5]

In a similar vein are the lines of Lucretius already cited :

Nec sic interemit mors res ut materiai
Corpora conficiat, sed coetum dissupat ollis,
Inde aliis aliud coniungit.[6]

---

[1] *Fr. 17 Schorn.*, Ritter et Preller, 119.
[2] *Pre-Socratic Philosophy*, II, p. 331. 1.
[3] II, p. 167.
[4] *Phys.*, I, 4, 187 a, 26, in Ritter et Preller, 120 a.
[5] *Plac.* V. 19, *Dox.* 430 a, in Ritter et Preller. 119 b.
[6] II. 1002-4.

On the same grounds which enable him to declare against generation and destruction, Anaxagoras asserts his belief in the unchangeableness of the sum of matter.

τούτων δὲ οὕτω διακεκριμένων γινώσκειν χρὴ, ὅτι πάντα οὐδὲν ἐλάσσω ἐστὶν οὐδὲ πλείω. οὐ γὰρ ἀνυστὸν πάντων πλείω εἶναι, ἀλλὰ πάντα ἴσα ἀεί.[1]

Epicurus has expressed himself with equal clearness and to the same effect :

καὶ μὴν καὶ τὸ πᾶν ἀεὶ τοιοῦτον ἦν οἷον νῦν ἐστι, καὶ ἀεὶ τοιοῦτον ἔσται. οὐθὲν γάρ ἐστιν εἰς ὃ μεταβαλεῖ. παρὰ γὰρ τὸ πᾶν οὐθέν ἐστιν, ὃ ἂν εἰσελθὸν εἰς αὐτὸ τὴν μεταβολὴν ποιήσαι.[2]

Lucretius has embodied the same teaching in lines already cited in connection with our discussion of Empedocles.[3]

That Lucretius had much sympathy with Anaxagoras will become further evident by an examination of a passage in the second book of the *De Rerum Natura*, in which there is a remarkably close translation of a fragment of the *Chrysippus* of Euripides, who was a disciple of Anaxagoras. A comparison of the corresponding passages in the two poets reveals the intimacy of Lucretius with the writings of Euripides, and implies some warmth of regard on the part of the latter for the former. Euripides says :

> Γαῖα μεγίστη καὶ Διὸς αἰθήρ,
> ὁ μὲν ἀνθρώπων καὶ θεῶν γενέτωρ,
> ἡ δ' ὑγροβόλους σταγόνας νοτίους
> παραδεξαμένη τίκτει θνατούς,
> τίκτει δὲ βορὰν, φῦλά τε θηρῶν
> ὅθεν οὐκ ἀδίκως
> μήτηρ πάντων νενόμισται.
> χωρεῖ δ' ὀπίσω τὰ μὲν ἐκ γαίας
> φύντ' εἰς γαῖαν, τὰ δ' ἀπ' αἰθερίου
> βλαστόντα γονῆς εἰς οὐράνιον
> πόλον ἦλθε πάλιν· θνήσκει δ' οὐδὲν
> τῶν γιγνομένων, διακρινόμενον δ'
> ἄλλο πρὸς ἄλλου
> μορφὴν ἰδίαν ἀπέδειξε.[4]

[1] Fr. 14 in Ritter et Preller, 120.
[2] *Diog. Laer.*, X. 39.
[3] II, 294-307. See p. 25.
[4] *Euripidis Fragmenta. Wagner Ed.*. Paris, 1878. Cf. Munro. II. p. 166.

The passage in Lucretius is as follows:

> *Denique caelesti sumus omnes semine oriundi;*
> *Omnibus ille idem pater est, unde alma liquentis*
> *Umoris guttas mater cum terra recepit,*
> *Feta parit nitidas fruges arbustaque laeta*
> *Et genus humanum, parit omnia saecla ferarum,*
> *Pabula cum praebet quibus omnes corpora pascunt*
> *Et dulcem ducunt vitam prolemque propagant;*
> *Quapropter merito maternum nomen adepta est.*
> *Cedit item retro, de terra quod fuit ante,*
> *In terras, et quod missumst ex aetheris oris,*
> *Id rursum caeli rellatum templa receptant.*
> *Nec sic interemit mors res ut materiai*
> *Corpora conficiat, sed coetum dissupat ollis,*
> *Inde aliis aliud coniungit.*[1]

Munro remarks that this "passage is quite Epicurean and consistent with the general argument of Lucretius, though his fondness for Euripides has made him express himself in the language of Anaxagoras."[2]

Another instance in which Lucretius has adapted the text of Anaxagoras to his own purpose is apparently afforded in one portion of his description of the manner in which the world was constructed. The declaration of Anaxagoras on the subject under consideration is:

τὸ μὲν πυκνὸν καὶ διερὸν καὶ ψυχρὸν καὶ τὸ ζοφερὸν ἐνθάδε συνεχώρησεν ἔνθα νῦν [ἡ γῆ]· τὸ δὲ ἀραιὸν καὶ τὸ θερμὸν καὶ τὸ ξηρὸν [καὶ τὸ λαμπρὸν] ἐξεχώρησεν εἰς τὸ πρόσω τοῦ αἰθέρος.[3]

> *Quippe etenim primum terrai corpora quaeque,*
> *Propterea quod erant gravia et perplexa, coibant*
> *In medio atque imas capiebant omnia sedes.*[4]

---

[1] II. 991-1004.
[2] Munro II. p. 166.
[3] Fr. 8. in Fairbank's *First Philosophers of Greece*. p. 242. Cf. Munro II. p. 306.
[4] V, 449-51.

The immediate occasion of conflict between Lucretius and Anaxagoras is the doctrine of the *homoeomeria* (ὁμοιομέρεια) or the theory that the parts of a body are altogether similar to the whole, and that these homogeneous parts are original and elementary substances, infinite in number and variety.[1] The account of this doctrine which Lucretius gives is comparatively brief, but is fair in the main and sufficiently exact for his purpose:

> *Principio, rerum quom dicit homoeomerian,*
> *Ossa videlicet e pauxillis atque minutis*
> *Ossibus hic et de pauxillis atque minutis*
> *Visceribus viscus gigni sanguenque creari*
> *Sanguinis inter se multis coeuntibu' guttis*
> *Ex aurique putat micis consistere posse*
> *Aurum et de terris terram concrescere parvis,*
> *Ignibus ex ignis, umorem umoribus esse,*
> *Cetera consimili fingit ratione putatque.*[2]

The argument which Lucretius makes against this doctrine will be considered after some examination of the actual teaching of Anaxagoras on this subject, as revealed in the most reliable extant sources of information.

The word homoeomeria (ὁμοιομέρεια) does not appear in the fragments of Anaxagoras which have been preserved to us. Is there any ground for supposing that he ever employed the term? On this question scholars are divided. Lucretius plainly asserts that Anaxagoras uses the word. Plutarch affirms the same:— Ὁμοιομερείας αὐτὰς ἐκάλεσε[2] Simplicius makes a like declaration:—

Ὅτι δὲ Ἀναξαγόρας ἐξ ἑνὸς μίγματος ἄπειρα τῷ πλήθει ὁμοιομερῆ ἀποκρίνεσθαί φησιν πάντων μὲν ἐν παντὶ ἐνόντων, ἑκάστου δὲ κατὰ τὸ ἐπικρατοῦν χαρακτηριζομένου, δηλοῖ διὰ τοῦ πρώτου τῶν Φυσικῶν λέγων ἀπ' ἀρχῆς.[3]

Munro unhesitatingly places himself in the company of those who attribute this word to Anaxagoras, and maintains that there is sufficient evidence that even this exact form of the word originated with him and not with Lucretius, as had at first seemed probable,

---

[1] I, 834-42.
[2] Munro, II p. 98.
[3] *Phys.* 33ᵛ 155, 23 D. Ritter et Preller, 120.

and as many critics still assert is the fact. Aristotle, who seems to be chiefly responsible for the perpetuation of the expression, it is admitted, never uses this substantive form (ὁμοιομερεία) but invariably the adjective (ὁμοιομερῆ). But Munro shows that he has himself traced the substantive to Epicurus, and expresses the conviction that, since Epicurus and his school were so well acquainted with Anaxagoras, they unquestionably derived it from them, and that Lucretius had it also from them and from Epicurus.[1]

Zeller, on the other hand, following Schleiermacher, Ritter and others, denies that the term was ever employed by Anaxagoras. He points in confirmation of this position not only to the fact that the term does not appear in the extant fragments of Anaxagoras, but also that in places where it would be natural to expect it, the words σπέρματα and χρήματα are found, and that the word cannot be satisfactorily explained except in connection with Aristotle's use of language, with whom he believes it originated; and contrary to Munro's assertion, which he may not have seen, declares that the word *homoeomeria* is first found in Lucretius.[2]

But whatever may have been the origin of the words ὁμοιομερεία and ὁμοιομερές, there is not a little doubt and confusion as to the precise meaning attaching to them. Aristotle himself is apparently not always consistent in his usage. In general terms he mantains that Anaxagoras claimed bodies of similar parts to be the elements of things, a plain reversal of the atomistic theory, which teaches that the organic is composed of the elementary and not the elementary of the constituents of the organic.[3] Ordinarily Aristotle employs the words τὸ ὁμοιομερεία, τὰ ὁμοιομερῆ to designate the whole whose parts are homogeneous with one another; in other words bodies which in all their parts consist of one and the same substance, in which, therefore, all parts are of like kind with one another and with the whole.

Ἀναξαγόρας δὲ ὁ Κλαζομένιος τῇ μὲν ἡλικίᾳ πρότερος ὢν τούτου (Ἐμπεδοκλέους), τοῖς δ' ἔργοις ὕστερος, ἀπείρους εἶναί φησι τὰς ἀρχάς· σχεδὸν γὰρ ἅπαντα τὰ ὁμοιομερῆ, καθάπερ ὕδωρ ἢ πῦρ, οὕτω γίγνεσθαι καὶ ἀπόλλυσθαί φησι συγκρι-

---
[1] Munro, II p. 98.
[2] Zeller, *Pre-Socratic Philosophy*, II. pp. 334, 35.
[3] *Ib.*, p. 334.

ANAXAGORAS. 39

σει καὶ διακρίσει μόνον, ἄλλως δ' οὔτε γίγνεσθαι οὔτ' ἀπόλλυσθαι, ἀλλὰ διαμένειν ἀΐδια.[1] But in other instances Aristotle evidently makes the words τὸ ὁμοιομερές and τὰ ὁμοιομερῆ refer to the homogeneous parts in distinction from the whole, as for example when he says:—

'Αναξαγόρας δ' 'Εμπεδοκλεῖ ἐναντίως λέγει περὶ τῶν στοιχείων. ὁ μὲν γὰρ πῦρ καὶ γῆν καὶ τὰ σύστοιχα τούτοις στοιχεῖά φησιν εἶναι τῶν σωμάτων καὶ συγκεῖσθαι πάντ' ἐκ τούτων, 'Αναξαγόρας δὲ τοὐναντίον. τὰ γὰρ ὁμοιομερῆ στοιχεῖα (λέγω δ' οἷον σάρκα καὶ ὀστοῦν καὶ τῶν τοιούτων ἕκαστον) ἀέρα δὲ καὶ πῦρ μῖγμα τούτων καὶ τῶν ἄλλων σπερμάτων πάντων·εἶναι γὰρ ἑκάτερον αὐτῶν ἐξ ἀοράτων ὁμοιομερῶν πάντων ἠθροισμένον.[2]

According to Zeller,[3] however, Aristotle is not to be regarded as seriously inconsistent, but as presenting a graduated scale of things under this terminology. At the bottom of the series are the primary elements. Next in order, and composed of the foregoing, are the bodies of similar parts. Finally we have the organic formed of the bodies of homogeneous parts. These last Aristotle designates by the term ἀνομοιομερῆ and they include the face, the hands, etc., bodies of unlike parts. The ὁμοιομερῆ include bone, flesh, gold, silver, etc., and these in turn are made of the smallest substances of the same kind as the bodies which they form. To represent these infinitesimal parts the plural of the substantive (ὁμοιομερείαι) is employed by later writers such as Plutarch, Diogenes Laertius and others, as Zeller, Ueberweg and others declare, but also by Epicurus, as has been proven, and perhaps by Anaxagoras himself, as Munro contends, though the extant fragments of Anaxagoras have only the words σπέρματα and χρήματα to designate the original constituents of things.

But in dealing with this subject it is contended that Anaxagoras did not mention elements, that term having been introduced into philosophy at a later period by Plato and Aristotle.[4] In short the primitive substances of Anaxagoras were infinitesimal bodies all of whose parts were homogeneous with one another. In the qualities which determined their distinctive characters they were underived and imperishable. Now the number of things which are not alike in the universe is unlimited. Hence there must be, according to

---
[1] Aristotle, *Met.* I, 3, 984 *a* 11. Ritter et Preller, 119 *a*.
[2] *De Caelo*, III, 3, 302 *a* 28. Ritter et Preller, 119 *a*.
[3] *Pre-Socratic Philosophy* II, p. 335, 3.
[4] *Ib.*, p. 126, 1.

Anaxagoras, an unlimited number of primordial bodies, not one of which resembles another, and these are differentiated in shape, color and taste.[1]

πρὶν δὲ ἀποκριθῆναι . . . - - πάντων ὁμοῦ ἐόντων οὐδὲ χροιὴ ἔνδηλος ἦν οὐδεμία. ἀπεκώλυε γὰρ ἡ σύμμιξις πάντων χρημάτων τοῦ τε διεροῦ καὶ τοῦ ξηροῦ καὶ τοῦ θερμοῦ καὶ τοῦ ψυχροῦ καὶ τοῦ λαμπροῦ καὶ τοῦ ζοφεροῦ καὶ γῆς πολλῆς ἐνεούσης καὶ σπερμάτων ἀπείρων πλήθους οὐδὲν ἐοικότων ἀλλήλοις. οὐδὲ γὰρ τῶν ἄλλων οὐδὲν ἔοικε τὸ ἕτερον τῷ ἑτέρῳ.[2]

τούτων δὲ οὕτως ἐχόντων, χρὴ δοκεῖν ἐνεῖναι πολλά τε καὶ παντοῖα ἐν πᾶσι τοῖς συγκρινομένοις καὶ σπέρματα πάντων χρημάτων καὶ ἰδέας παντοίας ἔχοντα καὶ χροιὰς καὶ ἡδονάς.[3]

The objections which Lucretius brings against Anaxagoras are characteristic. There is, of course, the fundamental difference between them at the very beginning, that the Epicureans posit one primitive matter, from which all things are derived by an infinite variety of combinations, while Anaxagoras maintains an unlimited number of primordial germs of every conceivable difference and quality. Out of this fundamental disagreement spring in the main the occasions of Lucretius' hostility.

The first count in the indictment against Anaxagoras is that he does not recognize void in his calculations of the process of combination and separation. Aristotle bears witness on this point as follows:—

οἱ μὲν οὖν δεικνύναι πειράμενοι ὅτι οὐκ ἔστιν (τὸ κενόν) οὐχ ὃ βούλονται λέγειν οἱ ἄνθρωποι κενόν, τοῦτ' ἐξελέγχουσιν ἀλλ' ἁμαρτάνοντες λέγουσιν, ὥσπερ Ἀναξαγόρας καὶ οἱ τοῦτον τὸν τρόπον ἐλέγχοντες, ἐπιδεικνύουσι γὰρ ὅτι ἔστι τι ὁ ἀὴρ στρεβλοῦντες τοὺς ἀσκοὺς καὶ δεικνύντες ὡς ἰσχυρὸς ὁ ἀὴρ καὶ ἐναπολαμβάνοντες ἐν ταῖς κλεψύδραις.[4]

In the second place Anaxagoras holds to the infinite divisibility of bodies, a position in direct conflict with the atomistic theory.

οὔτε γὰρ τοῦ σμικροῦ γε ἔστι τὸ γε ἐλάχιστον. ἀλλ' ἔλασσον ἀεί· τὸ γὰρ ἐὸν οὐκ ἔστι τὸ μὴ οὐκ εἶναι. ἀλλὰ καὶ τοῦ μεγάλου ἀεί ἐστι μεῖζον. καὶ ἴσον ἐστὶ τῷ σμικρῷ πλῆθος, πρὸς ἑαυτὸ δὲ ἕκαστόν ἐστι καὶ μέγα καὶ σμικρόν.[5]

---

[1] Zeller *Pre-Socratic Philosophy*, II, pp. 336, 37.
[2] *Fr.* 4, Ritter et Preller, 120. Cf. Fairbanks, *First Philosophers of Greece* p. 236.
[3] *Fr.* 3, Fairbanks, p. 236. Cf. Ritter et Preller, 120.
[4] *Phys.* VI, 6, 213 a 22. Ritter et Preller, 126.
[5] *Fr.* 15, Fairbanks, pp. 242, 44. Cf. Zeller, *Pre-Socratic Philosophy*, II p. 341, 3.

> *Quare in utraque mihi pariter ratione videtur*
> *Errare atque illi, supra quos diximus ante.*[1]

Again, primordia of the character ascribed to them by Anaxagoras will be too feeble in the judgment of Lucretius to withstand the shocks of antagonistic influences, and will ultimately perish.

> *Adde quod inbecilla nimis primordia fingit;*
> *Si primordia sunt, simili quae praedita constant*
> *Natura atque ipsae res sunt aequeque laborant*
> *Et pereunt neque ab exitio res ulla refrenat.*
> *Nam quid in oppressu valido durabit eorum,*
> *Ut mortem effugiat, leti sub dentibus ipsis?*
> *Ignis an umor an aura? quid horum? sanguen an ossa?*
> *Nil, ut opinor, ubi ex aequo res funditus omnis*
> *Tam mortalis erit quam quae manifesta videmus*
> *Ex oculis nostris aliqua vi victa perire.*

Such an obvious violation of the first principles of his philosophy cannot be tolerated by so earnest an Epicurean as Lucretius, who says:—

> *At neque reccidere ad nilum res posse neque autem*
> *Crescere de nilo testor res ante probatas.*[2]

Moreover, the fact that Anaxagoras attributes secondary qualities to his primitive particles is enough in the estimation of Lucretius to condemn the whole system. In his second book he labors ingeniously to demonstrate the impossibility that such qualities should belong to original matter. As these qualities are themselves destructible, he believes that the atoms possessing them would necessarily be perishable also.[3]

Again, Epicurus and his school argued that the atoms, though indivisible, consist of parts inseparable and undistinguishable, which have existed in the atoms from eternity. These are called by Epicurus ἐλάχιστοι and by Lucretius *minima*.

---

[1] I, 845-6.
[2] I, 847-58.
[3] II, 730-865.

τό τε ἐλάχιστον τὸ ἐν τῇ αἰσθήσει δεῖ κατανοεῖν ὅτι οὔτε τοιοῦτόν ἐστιν οἷον τὸ τὰς μεταβάσεις ἔχον οὔτε πάντῃ πάντως ἀνόμοιον,ἀλλ' ἔχον μέν τινα κοινότητα τῶν μεταβατῶν, διάληψιν δὲ μερῶν οὐκ ἔχον· ἀλλ' ὅταν διὰ τὴν τῆς κοινότητος προσεμφέρειαν οἰηθῶμεν διαλήψεσθαί τι αὐτοῦ, τὸ μὲν ἐπιτάδε, τὸ δὲ ἐπέκεινα, τὸ ἴσον ἡμῖν δεῖ προσπίπτειν. ἑξῆς τε θεωροῦμεν ταῦτα ἀπὸ τοῦ πρώτου καταρχόμενοι καὶ οὐκ ἐν τῷ αὐτῷ, οὐδὲ μέρεσι μερῶν, ἁπτόμεν', ἀλλ' ἢ ἐν τῇ ἰδιότητι τῇ ἑαυτῶν τά μεγέθη καταμετροῦντα, τὰ πλείω πλεῖον καὶ τὰ ἐλάττω ἔλαττον. ταύτῃ τῇ ἀναλογίᾳ νομιστέον καὶ τὸ ἐν τῇ ἀτόμῳ ἐλάχιστον κεχρῆσθαι. μικρότητι γὰρ ἐκεῖνο δῆλον ὡς διαφέρει τοῦ κατὰ τὴν αἴσθησιν θεωρουμένου, ἀναλογίᾳ δὲ τῇ αὐτῇ κέχρηται. ἐπεί περ καὶ ὅτι μέγεθος ἔχει ἡ ἄτομος, κατὰ τὴν [τῶν] ἐνταῦθα ἀναλογίαν κατηγορήσαμεν, μικρόν τι μόνον μακρὰν ἐκβάλλοντες.[1]

Lucretius has given considerable space to the discussion of these *minima*,[2] but Anaxagoras repudiates the whole idea. τοὐλάχιστον μὴ ἔστιν εἶναι.[3]

In harmony with all his reasoning, which is based on practical considerations, Lucretius interposes as objections to the doctrine of Anaxagoras a couple of dilemmas. In the first place,

. . . *quoniam cibus auget corpus alitque,*
Scire licet nobis venas et sanguen et ossa

. . . . . .

Sive cibos omnis commixto corpore dicent
Esse et habere in se nervorum corpora parva
Ossaque et omnino venas partisque cruoris,
Fiet uti cibus omnis, et aridus et liquor ipse,
Ex alienigenis rebus constare putetur,
Ossibus et nervis sanieque et sanguine mixto.[4]

In the second place,

. . . *quaecumque e terra corpora crescunt*
Si sunt in terris, terram constare necessest
Ex alienigenis, quae terris exoriuntur.
Transfer item, totidem verbis utare licebit.
In lignis si flamma latet fumusque cinisque,
Ex alienigenis consistant ligna necessest.

---

[1] *Diogenes Laertius*, X, 58, 59.
[2] I, 599-634.
[3] *Fr.* 16. Fairbanks, *First Philosophers of Greece*, p. 244.
[4] I, 859-66.

*Praeterea tellus quae corpora cumque alit, auget
Ex alienigenis, quae lignis his oriuntur.*[1]

In other words, inasmuch as food supports the body, it must contain particles of the same kind as the body, which are not the same kind as itself, or the body must include particles of the same kind as the food, but not of the same kind as itself. And the same reasoning applies to the production of plants out of the earth and the development of flames out of wood.

From these dilemmas Anaxagoras attempts to extricate himself by the hypothesis that all things are latent in each thing.

*Linquitur hic quaedam latitandi copia tenvis,
Id quod Anaxagoras sibi sumit, ut omnibus omnis
Res putet inmixtas rebus latitare, sed illud
Apparere unum cuius sint plurima mixta
Et magis in promptu primaque in fronte locata.*[2]

This representation of the position of Anaxagoras is certainly a fair one. He conceives all the primitive bodies as originally mixed together so throughly and in such infinitesimal particles that not one of them was individually perceptible, and therefore the combination exhibited none of the qualities of things in being.

ὁμοῦ χρήματα πάντα ἦν ἄπειρα καὶ πλῆθος καὶ σμικρότητα· καὶ γὰρ τὸ σμικρὸν ἄπειρον ἦν · καὶ πάντων ὁμοῦ ἐόντων οὐδὲν ἔνδηλον ἦν ὑπὸ σμικρότητος. πάντα γὰρ ἀήρ τε καὶ αἰθὴρ κατεῖχεν ἀμφότερα ἄπειρα ἐόντα · ταῦτα γὰρ μέγιστα ἔνεστιν ἐν τοῖσι σύμπασι καὶ πλήθεϊ καὶ μεγάθεϊ.[3]

But even things in being possessing all the qualities of the derived do not disclose the distinction between constituent bodies, but each contains parts of all; otherwise it would be impossible to explain the transition of all things into one another, and one could not come out of another, if it were not already a part of it.

ὁ μὲν ['Αναξαγόρας] ὁτιοῦν τῶν μορίων εἶναι μίγμα ὁμοίως τῷ παντὶ διὰ τὸ ὁρᾶν ὁτιοῦν ἐξ ὁτουοῦν γιγνόμενον · ἐντεῦθεν γὰρ ἔοικε καὶ ὁμοῦ ποτὲ πάντα χρήματα φάναι εἶναι, οἷον ἥδε ἡ σάρξ καὶ τόδε τὸ ὀστοῦν καὶ οὕτως ὁτιοῦν · καὶ πάντα ἄρα.

---

[1] I, 867-74.
[2] I, 875-79.
[3] Fr. 1 in Ritter et Preller. 120.

καὶ ἅμα τοίνυν · ἀρχὴ γὰρ οὐ μόνον ἐν ἑκάστῳ ἐστὶ τῆς διακρίσεως, ἀλλὰ καὶ πάντων κ. τ. λ.[1]

If, therefore, a thing seems to possess some single quality to the exclusion of others, it is simply because there is an excess of the substance indicated. The truth is that each thing has substances of every kind in it, but it derives its name from the predominating constituents, or as Munro puts it, "each individual thing is what it is by having in it the greatest number of ὁμοιομερῆ στοιχεῖα."[2]

Lucretius disposes of this theory quite summarily by answering that if it were true, corn, water, clods, wood etc., would when analyzed reveal vestiges of blood, milk, fire etc.; in other words when sufficiently divided they would exhibit traces of the substances fed to make them or produced from them. It is obvious that this is not the case, and we must conclude, decides Lucretius, that various things have certain elements in common.

His antagonist, he conjectures, may offer as an illustration of the opposite view the fact that tree-tops frequently catch fire by rubbing together under the action of the wind. But this simply demonstrates what he has already asserted, that there are many seeds of things which trees and heat possess in common. If there were fully formed particles of fire in trees or anything else they might burst into flame at any moment. It is all a matter of the arrangement and order of the *primordia* whether they form one thing or another.

Finally, Lucretius makes his favorite appeal to common sense, and closes his argument with a *reductio ad absurdum* which he evidently believes is unanswerable:

> *Denique iam quaecumque in rebus cernis apertis*
> *Si fieri non posse putas, quin materiai*
> *Corpora consimili natura praedita fingas,*
> *Hac ratione tibi pereunt primordia rerum:*
> *Fiet uti risu tremulo concussa cachinnent*
> *Et lacrimis salsis umectent ora genasque.*[3]

---

[1] Aristotle, *Phys.* III, 4, 203 a 23. Zeller *Pre-Socratic Phil.* II, 339, 1.
[2] II, p. 101.
[3] I, 915-20.

In the same vein are the verses of Lucretius in the second book (973–90), where he combats the idea that the atoms must be similar in quality to the whole, by showing that upon this supposition the atoms of men must be able to laugh and cry and moralize on their own constituent particles, and concludes,

> *Quod si delira haec furiosaque cernimus esse*
> *Et ridere potest non ex ridentibu' factus*
> *Et sapere et doctis rationem reddere dictis*
> *Non ex seminibus sapientibus atque disertis,*
> *Qui minus esse queant ea quae sentire videmus*
> *Seminibus permixta carentibus undique sensu?*

It has been remarked that there is a striking similarity between Lucretius' treatment of this portion of his argument against Anaxagoras, and the discussion on Empedocles in Book I, 803–29, both in language and matter. The reason for this is apparent. The particles of Anaxagoras seem to Lucretius to be open to the same criticism as the four elements of Empedocles. Both possess those secondary qualities which are the concomitants of things derived.[1]

In order to avoid blind Chance and eternal Necessity, Anaxagoras assumes Mind (νοῦς) as the world-forming energy, an immaterial essence which is the cause of all motion and order in the universe. This places him inevitably in opposition to the Epicurean doctrine of the fortuitous concourse of atoms, but as this speculation does not figure as a point of actual contention in the poem of Lucretius, we may properly leave it without treatment here.

3. Democritus.

It is natural to expect that Lucretius will treat Democritus with great gentleness and consideration on account of the unquestioned indebtedness of the Epicurean school to this philosopher. Epicurus can scarcely be said to have had any scientific attainments of his own,

---
[1] Munro, II, p. 102.

though he indulged in a superficial study of nature, and even ventured to publish the results of his investigations.[1] It is none the less true, however, that he would have looked with contempt upon all scientific observation but for the practical advantages which such study afforded him in his attempt to destroy the baneful influences of superstition on the human mind.[2] For any other purpose the labor involved would have been esteemed superfluous by him. Science, therefore, Epicurus held to be subsidiary to ethics. Let the searcher after truth take whatever explanation of physical phenomena he will— only in the name of reason and for the sake of human comfort let him not attribute them to the interference of divine hands—is the doctrine of Epicurus.

Some general mechanical theory, however, is necessary to account for the world and its activities, in order to banish this delusion of the human race. Now, the atomic theory of Leucippus and Democritus best serves Epicurus in this regard, and he adopts it without making any contribution to it except in a single instance, which will be mentioned hereafter.

The dependence of Epicurus upon Democritus did not escape the keen scrutiny of Cicero, who says: *Quid est in physicis Epicuri non a Democrito? Nam etsi quaedam commutauit ut quod paullo ante de inclinatione atomorum dixi, tamen pleraque dicit eadem, atomos inane imagines, infinitatem locorum innumerabilitatemque mundorum, eorum ortus interitus, omnia fere quibus naturae ratio continetur.*[3] *In physicis, quibus maxime gloriatur, primum totus est alienus (Epicurus). Democritea dicit perpauca mutans, sed ita ut ea quae corrigere uolt, mihi quidem depruare uideatur . . ita quae mutat ea corrumpit, quae sequitur sunt tota Democriti . . . quae etsi mihi nullo probantur, tamen Democritum laudatum a ceteris ab hoc, qui eum unum secutus esset,*

---

[1] Thirty-seven books entitled περὶ φύσεως, mentioned by Diogenes Laertius, X, 27.

[2] εἰ μηθὲν ἡμᾶς αἱ τῶν μετεώρων ὑποψίαι ἠνώχλουν καὶ αἱ περὶ θανάτου, μή ποτε πρὸς ἡμᾶς ᾖ τι, ἔτι τε τὸ μὴ κατανοεῖν τοὺς ὅρους τῶν ἀλγηδόνων καὶ τῶν ἐπιθυμιῶν, οὐκ ἂν προσεδεόμεθα φυσιολογίας. *Diog. Laer.* X, 142. Usener, *Epicurea*, p. 74.

[3] *De Natura Deorum*, I, 26, 72.

*nollem uituperatum.*¹ . . *Democritus, uir magnus in primis, cuius fontibus Epicurus hortulos suos inrigauit.*²

In the same vein is the testimony of Plutarch:³ Δημοκρίτου καλὰ καὶ πρέποντα διδασκάλια κομιζομένου παρ' αὐτοῦ ('Επικούρου), and Diogenes Laertius records: φησὶ δ' Έρμιππος γραμματοδιδάσκαλον αὐτὸν γεγενῆσθαι, ἔπειτα μέντοι περιτυχόντα τοῖς Δημοκρίτου βιβλίοις, ἐπὶ φιλοσοφίαν ᾆξαι.⁴ Usener has pointed out many positive imitations of Democritus in the writings of Epicurus.⁵ Notwithstanding these palpable evidences of the heavy indebtedness of Epicurus, he was very slow to acknowledge that he was under obligation to any teacher. He loved to herald himself as untaught.⁶ He refrained from praising even those from whom he had undoubtedly derived instruction. Cicero, referring to the custom of Socrates to eulogize other philosophers, says: *Decet hoc nescio quo modo illum, nec Epicuro, qui id reprehendit, assentior.*⁷ Diogenes Laertius also remarks:

ἀλλ' οὐδὲ Λεύκιππόν τινα γεγενῆσθαί φησι φιλόσοφον,οὔτε αὐτὸς οὔτε Έρμαρχος, ὃν ἔνιοί φασι καὶ 'Απολλόδωρος ὁ 'Επικούρειος διδάσκαλον Δημοκρίτου γεγενῆσθαι.⁸

This fully justifies Cicero's accusation of ingratitude.⁹ At the same time Epicurus somewhat reluctantly gave an occasional acknowledgment of his association with the Democritean school.

καί τοι πολὺν χρόνον αὐτὸς ἑαυτὸν ἀνηγόρευε Δημοκρίτειον ὁ 'Επίκουρος,ὡς ἄλλοι τε λέγουσι καὶ Λεοντεύς, εἷς τῶν ἐπ' ἄκρον 'Επικούρου μαθητῶν, πρὸς Λυκόφρονα γράφων τιμᾶσθαί τέ φησι τὸν Δμμόκριτον ὑπ' 'Επικούρου διὰ τὸ πρότερον ἅψασθαι τῆς ὀρθῆς γνώσεως, καὶ τὸ σύνολον τὴν πραγματείαν Δημοκρίτειον προσαγορεύεσθαι διὰ τὸ περιπεσεῖν αὐτὸν πρότερον ταῖς ἀρχαῖς περὶ φύσεως.¹⁰

---

¹*De Finibus* I, 6, 17, 21.
²*De Natura Deorum* I, 43, 120.
³Usener, *Epicurea*, p. 175.
⁴X, 3. Usener, p. 360.
⁵*Epicurea*, p. 402.
⁶*De Natura Deorum* I, 26, 72.
⁷*Brutus*, 85, 292.
⁸X, 13.
⁹*De Natura Deorum* I, 33, 93.
¹⁰Plutarch in Usener, *Epicurea*, p. 175.

However, he treated Democritus himself, in at least one instance, with undisguised contempt.¹ Lucretius shows a far more commendable spirit than Epicurus in relation to Democritus. He makes no attempt to conceal his unqualified admiration for the philosopher to whom he owes so much. It is characteristic of Lucretius that, while he discredits all gods, he sets up for worship the best substitute he can find—a hero, to whom he can conscientiously pay divine honor. His enthusiasm for great men not only leads him to venerate Epicurus as a god, but also to be exceedingly deferential to every commanding figure. To Epicurus he assigns the supremacy among men, but Empedocles, Ennius, Homer, Democritus and others are entitled to lofty positions in his pantheon. Democritus would seem to occupy the closest proximity to Epicurus, if there is any significance in the arrangement of the names in the striking passage in which he strives to mitigate the terrors of death by celebrating the fact that the grandest characters in human history have been compelled to undergo the same melancholy experience:

Denique Democritum postquam matura vetustas
Admonuit memores motus languescere mentis,
*Sponte sua leto cuput obvius optulit ipse.*²

The pressure of Democritus upon Lucretius is amply manifest. One of the most concise presentations of the doctrines of Democritus which we possess is that given by Diogenes Laertius. A comparison of the physical theories of Lucretius with the statements of Democritus on corresponding questions contained in the following passage, will reveal the close affiliation of the two authors:

Ἀρχὰς εἶναι τῶν ὅλων ἀτόμους, καὶ κενόν· τὰ δ' ἄλλα πάντα νενομίσθαι δοξάζεσθαι. Ἀπείρους τε εἶναι κόσμους, καὶ γενητοὺς, καὶ φθαρτούς. Μηδὲν τε ἐκ τοῦ μὴ ὄντος γίνεσθαι, μηδὲ εἰς τὸ μὴ ὂν φθείρεσθαι. Καὶ τὰς ἀτόμους δὲ ἀπείρους εἶναι κατὰ μέγεθος καὶ πλῆθος· φέρεσθαι δ' ἐν τῷ ὅλῳ δινουμένας. Καὶ οὕτω πάντα τὰ συγκρίματα γεννᾶν, πῦρ, ὕδωρ, ἀέρα, γῆν. Εἶναι γὰρ καὶ ταῦτα ἐξ ἀτόμων τινῶν συστήματα· ἅπερ εἶναι ἀπαθῆ καὶ ἀναλλοίωτα διὰ τὴν στερρότητα. Τόν τε ἥλιον καὶ τὴν σελήνην ἐκ τοιούτων δινῶν καὶ περιφερῶν ὄγκων συγκεκρίσθαι, καὶ τὴν ψυχὴν ὁμοίως· ἣν καὶ νοῦν ταὐτὸν εἶναι. Ὁρᾶν δ' ἡμᾶς κατ' εἰδώλων ἐμπτώσεις.³

---
¹*Diogenes Laertius* X, 8.
² III, 1039-1041.
³*Diogenes Laertius* IX, 44.

It will be seen by this declaration of the Democritean principles that Lucretius has much in common with their author. They agree on the origin of the universe; the solidity, indivisibility and eternity of the atoms; the materiality of the soul; the media of sense perceptions and other points of importance to be indicated hereafter. Special interest centres in the doctrine of emanations as held by Lucretius and Democritus.[1] In the scheme of the latter this theory plays a more important part than in that of the former. According to Democritus not only vision, but all perception, both that of the senses and of thought itself, has its origin in these emanations, which penetrate into the body through the organs of sense, and thus spreading through all its parts, produce a representation of things. But to secure this result it is essential that the emanations shall be like the organs of the body in material constitution. We perceive each thing with that part of our nature whick is akin to it. Democritus differed from Lucretius and Empedocles on the method of sense perception in this particular, that he did not conceive of his emanations as coming into direct contact with the organs of the body. The space between the objects and our bodies is filled with air. The εἴδωλα, therefore, cannot themselves reach our senses, but the air which is moved by them does so. Clearness of perception naturally decreases in proportion to the distance between the organs of sense and the image to be reproduced to sight, or the source from which sound emanates or thought proceeds. It is evident that with such a view of the mode of communicating impressions, there can be no accuracy of knowledge through perception. And as thought is declared by Democritus to have a similar origin, it is difficult to see how he can place any more reliance upon the phenomena of the mind than upon the sensations of the body, though he doubtless does.[2] To the doctrine of emanations held by Lucretius, Empedocles, Democritus and Epicurus each contributed a part, the last named having had an especial influence upon the poet.[3] From the

---

[1] Λεύκιππος Δημόκριτος τὴν αἴσθησιν καὶ τὴν νόησιν γίνεσθαι εἰδώλων ἔξωθεν προσιόντων · μηδενὶ γὰρ ἐπιβάλλειν μηδετέραν χωρὶς τοῦ προσπίπτοντος εἰδώλου. *Plac.* IV, 8. *Dox.* 395 in Ritter et Preller, 155.
[2] Zeller, *Pre-Socratic Philosophy*, II, pp. 265-72.
[3] Cf. *Diogenes Laertius* X. 46-53, with *Lucretius*, IV.

surface of all bodies infinitesimal particles are streaming every moment. These particles take the figure of the objects from which they proceed, and thus form images or *idola* of the things they leave. These emanations are spontaneously generated, they are incessantly streaming, they move with almost inconceivable rapidity, and should they cease at any time we should at once lose sight, smell and hearing. By reason of this perpetual evaporation of matter a never-ending waste is going on, which explains the theory of Lucretius that the world is continually being fed with fresh matter from without. Moreover, on account of the porosity of matter, these *simulacra* constantly pass through them in all directions. Thus all bodies are to a greater or less degree interpenetrated with other matter. Somewhat more obscurely, but none the less truly, does Lucretius state the Empedoclean notion of pores differing from or resembling in shape the atoms which proceed by this streaming process from all bodies.[1] To these emanations we are indebted for dreams, apparitions and many other strange phenomena. Our conceptions of the deities, for example, have their origin in these images. But while Democritus distrusts the evidences of the senses, Lucretius, as we have already seen, maintains the absolute correctness of the presentations of these organs of perception. If misconceptions are formed from the testimony of the senses, it must be the mind which errs in the inferences made.[2]

There is a striking similarity in the views expressed by Lucretius and Democritus on the question of the *summum bonum*, although there is an unimportant difference in the terms employed.

Τέλος δὲ εἶναι τὴν εὐθυμίαν, οὐ τὴν αὐτὴν οὖσαν τῇ ἡδονῇ, ὡς ἔνιοι παρακούσαντες ἐξεδέξαντο, ἀλλὰ καθ' ἣν γαληνῶς καὶ εὐσταθῶς ἡ ψυχὴ διάγει, ὑπὸ μηδενὸς ταραττομένη φόβου, ἢ δεισιδαιμονίας, ἢ ἄλλου τινὸς πάθους. Καλεῖ δ' αὐτὴν καὶ εὐεστώ, καὶ πολλοῖς ἄλλοις ὀνόμασι.[3]

If we compare this declaration with all that has been preserved as the doctrine of Epicurus upon the same subject, we shall find that the difference between the two is virtually nothing. In the recorded sayings of Epicurus there is surely as refined a conception of the

---
[1] Masson, *Atomic Theory of Lucretius*, p. 46.
[2] *Lucretius*, IV, 379–86.
[3] *Diogenes Laertius*, IX, 45.

meaning and function of pleasure as has been anywhere expressed by Democritus so far as our knowledge of his sentiments enables us to judge.[1] Lucretius, who follows Epicurus faithfully here as elsewhere, expresses himself with equal dignity and forcefulness:

> *O miseras hominum mentes, O pectora caeca!*
> *Qualibus in tenebris vitae quantisque periclis*
> *Degitur hoc aevi quodcumquest! nonne videre*
> *Nil aliud sibi naturam latrare, nisi ut qui*
> *Corpore seiunctus dolor absit, mente fruatur*
> *Iucundo sensu cura semota metuque?*
> *Ergo corpoream ad naturam pauca videmus*
> *Esse opus omnino, quae demant cumque dolorem.*
> *Delicias quoque uti multas substernere possint*
> *Gratius interdum, neque natura ipsa requirit,*
> *Si non aurea sunt iuvenum simulacra per aedes*
> *Lampadas igniferas manibus retinentia dextris,*
> *Lumina nocturnis epulis ut suppeditentur,*
> *Nec domus argento fulget auroque renidet*
> *Nec citharae reboant laqueata aurataque tecta,*
> *Cum tamen inter se prostrati in gramine molli*
> *Propter aquae rivum sub ramis arboris altae*
> *Non magnis opibus iucunde corpora curant,*
> *Praesertim cum tempestas adridet et anni*
> *Tempora conspergunt viridantis floribus herbas.*
> *Nec calidae citius decedunt corpore febres,*
> *Textilibus si in picturis ostroque rubenti*
> *Iacteris, quam si in plebeia veste cubandum est.*
> *Quapropter quoniam nil nostro in corpore gazae*
> *Proficiunt neque nobilitas nec gloria regni*
> *Quod super est, animo quoque nil prodesse putandum.*[2]

In this connection we may also note the similarity of attitude which Democritus and Lucretius take with reference to the passion of love. For sexual enjoyment they both have a certain contempt,

---

[1] *Diogenes Laertius*, X. 128–132, 140. Usener, *Epicurea*, pp. 62–64. 72.
[2] II, 14–39.

which in Democritus amounts to positive hatred, because in the persuit of such pleasure the man gives himself over to the degrading charm of the senses.[1] The intense earnestness of Lucretius in dealing with this subject in the fourth book of his poem, seems almost like a commentary on the creed of Democritus in this regard.

An illustration of the characteristic Epicurean method of accounting for physical phenomena is afforded in the passage on earthquakes in the sixth book, where Lucretius, following his master, is in accord with Democritus in assigning these disturbances to a variety of causes. Epicurus, after specifying certain reasons for earthquakes, naively says: καὶ κατ' ἄλλους δὲ πλείους τρόπους τὰς κινήσεις ταύτας τῆς γῆς γίνεσθαι.[2]

We are indebted to Seneca for what Munro calls a better illustration of Lucretius in this connection than the extant writings of Epicurus himself provide, since the larger works of the latter, which Lucretius had no means of consulting, were available to Seneca, who says: *Veniamus nunc ad eos qui omnia ista quae rettuli in causa esse dixerunt aut ex his plura. Democritus plura putat. Ait enim motum aliquando spiritu fieri, aliquando aqua, aliquando utroque. . . . Omnes istas posse esse causas Epicurus ait pluresque alias temptat et alios qui aliquid unum ex istis esse adfirmaverunt corripit, etc.* (*Nat. Quaest.* VI, 20.)[3] Attention has already been called to the fact that palpable imitations of Democritus have been attributed to Epicurus. It has also been maintained that Lucretius made liberal use of the same authority. The words *ordo, positura, figurae*, which appear in the same succession and with the same technical significance in I, 685 and II, 1021, have been traced to Democritus, by whom their Greek equivalents were employed according to the testimony of two authorities. Aristotle says:

Δημοκρίτῳ μὲν οὖν τρεῖς διαφορὰς ἔοικεν οἰομένῳ εἶναι· τὸ μὲν γὰρ ὑποκείμενον σῶμα τὴν ὕλην ἓν καὶ ταὐτόν, διαφέρειν δὲ ἢ ῥυσμῷ ὅ ἐστι σχῆμα, ἢ τροπῇ ὅ ἐστι θέσις, ἢ διαθιγῇ ὅ ἐστι τάξις.[4]

---

[1] Zeller, *Pre-Socratic Philosophy*, II, p. 285.
[2] *Diogenes Laertius* X, 105, 106.
[3] Munro, II, p. 370.
[4] *Metaph.*, VIII, 2, p. 1042, b. 11. Munro, II, p. 87.

Simplicius, referring to the doctrines of Democritus, says: τρεῖς δέ εἰσιν αὗται ῥυσμὸς τροπὴ διαθιγή, ταὐτὸν δὲ εἰπεῖν σχῆμα καὶ θέσις καὶ τάξις.[1]

The theory that Lucretius enjoyed an intimate acquaintance with the writings of Democritus must not be pressed too far, however, since in all probability the philosopher of Abdera was better known to later writers than to Lucretius and his contemporaries. Two generations after the *De Rerum Natura* was published, in the era of Tiberius, Thrasylus wrote an introduction to the writings of the famous atomist.

τὰ δὲ βιβλία αὐτοῦ καὶ Θρασύλος ἀναγέγραφε κατὰ τάξιν οὕτως ὥσπερεὶ καὶ τὰ Πλάτωνος, κατὰ τετραλογίαν, says Diogenes Laertius.[2] It is apparent that in the study of Democritus the opportunities of Lucretius did not equal those of his successors.

But while Lucretius agrees in many of the principles of his philosophy with Democritus and offers similar elucidations of physical phenomena, he does not hesitate to differ from him in important particulars. The most significant divergence between the positions of these two men is found in the celebrated passage on the declination of the atoms in the second book. The doctrine of Democritus concerning the origin of motion and the subsequent formation of the visible universe is attacked with firmness but courtesy. Doubtless the admiration of Lucretius for Democritus impelled him to treat a subject, which he knew to be of the utmost significance to his system, with far more considerateness for his rival than he was accustomed to show toward opponents. The early atomists, of whom Leucippus and Democritus are the representative figures, explained the facts of nature neither on the ground of chance nor of design, but referred them to natural and necessary causes. Starting with the postulate which the Epicureans adopted, that atoms and the void constitute the whole of nature, they sought the origin of motion in gravitation. The weight of the atoms, they declared, is the eternal cause of their movement. The velocity with which these atoms proceed through space is conditioned on their mass. The larger and the

---

[1] Ritter et Preller, *Hist. Phil. Graecae*, 148 B.
[2] IX. 45.

heavier naturally fall with greater swiftness than the smaller and lighter. They stream down through the void in perpendicular lines, but the rapidity with which the heavy atoms descend enables them to overtake and impinge on the lighter and slower ones, in consequence of which there are deflections and repulsions, which set up at length a rotary movement of matter from which was evolved the entire order of the universe.[1] That by means of collisions and interminglings the worlds and all they contain were produced, is the doctrine of Epicurus no less than of Democritus; but there is a fundamental difference in their respective methods of accounting for the beginnings of the process. And Lucretius has presented the arguments against the Democritean hypothesis with great force.

The first reason adduced by the poet for rejecting the theory of Democritus is that it is inadequate to the task of accounting for the existence of the universe, being founded upon a false physical proposition. For the statement that the heavier atoms will ultimately strike the lighter in their perpendicular plunge through space is invalidated by the fact that in a vacuum all bodies move with the same rapidity.

> *Quod si forte aliquis credit graviora potesse*
> *Corpora, quo citius rectum per inane feruntur,*
> *Incidere ex supero levioribus atque ita plagas*
> *Gignere quae possint genitalis reddere motus,*
> *Avius a vera longe ratione recedit.*
> *Nam per aquas quaecumque cadunt atque aera rarum,*
> *Haec pro ponderibus casus celerare necessest*
> *Propterea quia corpus aquae naturaque tenvis*
> *Aeris haut possunt aeque rem quamque morari,*
> *Sed citius cedunt gravioribus exsuperata;*
> *At contra nulli de nulla parte neque ullo*
> *Tempore inane potest vacuum subsistere rei,*
> *Quin, sua quod natura petit, concedere pergat;*
> *Omnia, quapropter debent per inane quietum*

---

[1] οἱ περὶ Δημόκριτον καὶ ὕστερον Ἐπίκουρος τὰς ἀτόμους πάσας ὁμοφυεῖς οὔσας βάρος ἔχειν φασί, τῷ δὲ εἶναί τινα βαρύτερα ἐξωθούμενα τὰ κουφότερα ὑπ' αὐτῶν ὑφιζανόντων ἐπὶ τὸ ἄνω φέρεσθαι· καὶ οὕτω λέγουσιν οὗτοι δοκεῖν τὰ μὲν κοῦφα εἶναι τὰ δὲ βαρέα. Simplicius in Ritter et Preller, 149 e.

*Aeque ponderibus non aequis concita ferri.
Haud igitur poterunt levioribus incidere umquam
Ex supero graviora neque ictus gignere per se
Qui varient motus per quos natura gerat res.*[1]

In arguing the equal rapidity of the atoms through space and the consequent impossibility of atom overtaking atom in the eternal descent, and thus rendering generation and combination inconceivable without some variation of the downward sweep or the interference of the divine will, which he distinctly disavows, Lucretius follows Epicurus, who says:

καὶ μὴν καὶ ἰσοταχεῖς ἀναγκαῖον τὰς ἀτόμους εἶναι, ὅταν διὰ τοῦ κενοῦ εἰσφέρωνται μηθενὸς ἀντικόπτοντος. οὔτε γὰρ τὰ βαρέα θᾶττον οἰσθήσεται τῶν μικρῶν καὶ κούφων, ὅταν γε δὴ μηδὲν ἀπαντᾷ αὐτοῖς· οὔτε τὰ μικρὰ [βραδύτερον] τῶν μεγάλων, πάντα πόρον σύμμετρον ἔχοντα, ὅταν μηθὲν μηδὲ ἐκείνοις ἀντικόπτῃ.[2]

To account for the collision of the atoms and the resultant combination of matter and the formation of the worlds and their contents, Lucretius and Epicurus adopt an ingenious expedient.

*Corpora cum deorsum rectum per inane feruntur
Ponderibus propriis, se incerto tempore ferme
Incertisque locis spatio depellere paulum,
Tantum quod momen mutatum dicere possis.
Quod nisi declinare solerent, omnia deorsum,
Imbris uti guttae, caderent per inane profundum,
Nec foret offensus natus nec plaga creata
Principiis: ita nil umquam natura creasset.*[3]

Lucretius seems to have realized how dangerous a thing it was to introduce this physical contrivance into his system, for he attempts to guard his readers from the error of supposing that the atoms can travel downward in oblique lines, as would be the case if the swerve were more than the slightest conceivable variation from the perpendicular.

---

[1] II, 225-42.
[2] *Diogenes Laertius* X, 61. This objection, it is asserted, was borrowed from Aristotle. Cf. Zeller, *Stoics, Epicureans and Sceptics*, p. 445, 5. Masson *Atomic Theory of Lucretius*, p. 48.
[3] II, 217-24.

> *Quare etiam atque etiam paulum inclinare necessest*
> *Corpora; nec plus quam minimum, ne fingere motus*
> *Obliquos videamur et id res vera refutet..*
> *Namque hoc in promptu manifestumque esse videmus,*
> *Pondera, quantum in sest, non posse obliqua meare,*
> *Ex supero cum praecipitant, quod cernere possis;*
> *Sed nil omnino recta regione viai*
> *Declinare quis est qui possit cernere sese?* [1]

It also seems apparent from the phraseology employed that Lucretius conceived his atoms as swerving from their own inner impulse, the words *se depellere* especially pointing to this conclusion.[2]

The testimony of Cicero as a student of Epicureanism, though he ridicules the expedient, is valuable in this connection as to the belief of that school in the necessity of using the swerve to account for combination and generation, and also as to their faith in the inherent tendency of the atoms to diverge almost imperceptibly by their own impulse:

> *Epicurus autem in quibus sequitur Democritum, non fere labitur . . . illae Epicuri propriae ruinae censet: enim eadem illa indiuidua et solida corpora ferri deorsum suo pondere ad lineam, hunc naturalem esse omnium corporum motum. Deinde ibidem homo acutus, cum illud occurreret, si omnia deorsus e regione ferrentur et ut dixi ad lineam, nunquam fore ut atomus altera alteram posset attingere itaque . . attulit rem commenticiam; declinare dixit atomum perpaullum, quo nihil posset fieri minus; ita effici complexiones et copulationes et adhaesiones atomorum inter se, ex quo efficeretur mundus omnesque partes mundi quaeque in eo essent. Quae cum res tota ficta sit pueriliter, tum ne efficit quidem, quod vult. Nam et ipsa declinatio ad libidinem fingitur (ait enim declinare atomum sine causa; quo nihil turpius physico, quam fieri quicquam sine causa dicere), et illum motum naturalem omnium ponderum, ut ipse constituit, e regione inferiorem locum petentium sine causa eripuit atomis nec tamen id, cuius causa haec finxerat, assecutus est. Nam si omnes atomi declinabunt, nullae umquam cohaerescent, sive aliae declinabunt, aliae suo nutu recte ferentur, primum erit hoc quasi provincias atomis dare, quae recte,*

---

[1] II, 243-50.
[2] Munro, II, p. 132.

quae oblique ferantur, deinde eadem illa atomorum, in quo etiam Democritus haeret, turbulenta concursio hunc mundi ornatum efficere non poterit.[1]

But not only does the doctrine of the swerve enable Lucretius to explain the contact of the atoms in space, but it also serves a far more important purpose. It affords a rational basis for the doctrine of free will, which the Epicureans maintained against the Stoics, the early Atomists and other schools of thought. If the atoms had no power to decline, neither would men, constructed by a fortuitous concourse of these atoms, have the ability to move at will. The power of declination in the atoms corresponds to free action in animals and men, and according to Lucretius the former is the cause of the latter. It has been conjectured that had not Lucretius required this theory to explain the mystery of free will, he would have left his whirling atoms to take care of themselves, nor bothered his soul over the process of world formation. But the desire to avoid the doctrine of eternal necessity or fate impelled him to invent this method of accounting for the freedom of the will.[2] Here Lucretius again followed his master, Epicurus, who—*cum videret, si atomi ferrentur in locum inferiorem suopte pondere, nihil fore in nostra potestate, quod esset earum motus certus et necessarius, invenit quo modo necessitatem effugeret, quod videlicet Democritum fugerat; ait atomum, cum pondere et gravitate derecto deorsus feratur, declinare paullulum.*[3] . . . *Epicurus declinatione atomi vitari necessitatem fati putat. Itaque tertius quidam motus oritur extra pondus et plagam, cum declinat atomus intervallo minimo—id appellat* ἐλάχιστον—; *quam declinationem sine causa fieri si minus verbis, re cogitur confiteri.* . . . *Hanc Epicurus rationem induxit ob eam rem, quod veritus est ne si semper atomus gravitate ferretur naturali ac necessaria, nihil liberum nobis esset, cum ita moveretur animus, ut atomorum motu cogeretur. Id Democritus auctor atomorum accipere maluit, necessitate omnia fieri, quam a corporibus individuis naturalis motus avellere.*[4]

Epicurus doubtless did adopt the hypothesis of the declination or swerve—as Cicero declares—in order to avoid the Democritean

---

[1] Cicero, *De Finibus.* I, 6, 18-20.
[2] Munro, II, p. 136.
[3] Cicero, *De Natura Deorum*, I. 25, 69.
[4] Cicero, *De Fato*, 10, 22, 23.

doctrine of eternal necessity. He has emphatically denounced this teaching in his famous letter to Menaeceus, and despite his purpose to remove the gods from all participation in human affairs, he says:

κρεῖττον ἦν τῷ περὶ θεῶν μύθῳ κατακολουθεῖν ἢ τῇ τῶν φυσικῶν εἱμαρμένῃ δουλεύειν.[1]

This conviction Lucretius seems to share.

The adoption of the swerve is from the standpoint of Cicero a thoroughly absurd, if not dishonest, proceeding. He cannot admit that the conceit is rational. *Declinat, inquit, atomus. Primum cur? Aliam enim quandam vim motus habebant a Democrito inpulsionis, quam plagam ille appellat, a te, Epicure, gravitatis et ponderis. Quae ergo nova causa in natura est qua declinet atomus? Aut num sortiuntur inter se, quae declinet, quae non? Aut cur minimo declinent intervallo, maiore non? Aut cur declinent uno minimo, non declinent duobus aut tribus? Optare hoc quidem est, non disputare. Nam neque extrinsecus inpulsam atomum loco moveri et declinare dicis, neque in illo inani, per quod feratur atomus, quicquam fuisse causae, cur ea non e regione ferretur, nec in ipsa atomo mutationis aliquid factum est, quam ob rem naturalem motum sui ponderis non teneret. Ita cum attulisset nullam causam, quae istam declinationem efficeret, tamen aliquid sibi dicere videtur, cum id dicat quod omnium mentes aspernentur ac respuant.*[2]

Nec . . . est causa cur Epicurus fatum extimescat et ab atomis petat praesidium easque de via deducat et uno tempore suscipiat res duas inenodabiles, unam, ut sine causa fiat aliquid—ex quo existet ut de nihilo quippiam fiat . . ., alteram, ut cum duo individua per inanitatem ferantur, alterum e regione moveatur, alterum declinet.[3]

Of course in this asumption of the doctrine of free will Lucretius antagonizes the Stoics, of whom Plutarch says in this relation:

Ἐπικούρῳ μὲν γὰρ οὐδ' ἀκαρὲς ἐγκλῖναι τὴν ἄτομον συγχωροῦσιν (οἱ Στωικοί) ὡς ἀναίτιον ἐπεισάγοντι κίνησιν ἐκ τοῦ μὴ ὄντος.[4]

But of the conflict with this school we are to speak at some length

---

[1] *Diogenes Laertius.* X, 134.
[2] *De Fato,* 20, 46.
[3] *Ib.* 9, 18.
[4] *De Animae Procreatione in Tim. Plat.* Usener. p. 201.

later. It is of some significance, however, to observe at this point that Cicero approaches more closely to the school which denies free will than to the defenders of this doctrine, though he maintains a theory of fate or destiny which is in virtual accord with the highest conceptions of Providence, defending on the one hand the decrees of Deity and on the other the qualified liberty of man. He commends Democritus for adhering to the doctrine of necessity as being consistent with his physical hypothesis,[1] and does not hesitate to declare that Epicurus is devoid of judgment. Referring to the expedient of the swerve, he says: *Hoc dicere turpius est quam illud, quod vult, non posse defendere.*[2]

Carneades, he asserts, has produced a far better method of accounting for free will. *Acutius Carneades, qui docebat posse Epicureos suam causam sine hac commenticia declinatione defendere. Nam cum docerent esse posse quendam animi motum voluntarium, id fuit defendi melius quam introducere declinationem . . . Cum enim concessissent motum nullum esse sine causa, non concederent omnia quae fierent, fieri causis antecedentibus; voluntatis enim nostrae non esse causas externas et antecedentis.*[3]

But the argument which Lucretius makes in behalf of free will is worthy of respectful attention despite the fact that Cicero, Plutarch and other writers ridiculed the Epicurean expedient. For there is no more serious piece of reasoning in the entire poem than that which Lucretius devotes to the theory of atomic declination. The philosophy of Epicurus has emancipated him from slavery to that superstition, which attributes to the deities interference with the affairs of men, and from the fear of unseen powers which is consequent upon this delusion. But he has no sooner escaped from this terror than he is confronted by an equally forbidding phantom—eternal necessity or fate, which annuls the free action of men and reduces them to mere machines of destiny. If the universe is the product of relentless law, each process following a fixed and unalterable order, cause upon cause, motion upon motion, in everlasting and unbroken sequence, then there can not possibly be any free will. How to elude, on the

---

[1] *De Fato, passim.*
[2] *De Natura Deorum,* I. 25, 70.
[3] *De Fato,* 11, 23.

one hand, the tyranny of the gods and, on the other, the thralldom of necessity, is the problem which was presented to Epicurus, and the swerve was to him a sufficient solution of the puzzle. Without this device he cannot account, from his point of view, for the freedom of the human will. Lucretius fairly exposes the difficulty—

> *Denique si semper motus conectitur omnis*
> *Et vetere exoritur semper novus ordine certo*
> *Nec declinando faciunt primordia motus*
> *Principium quoddam quod fati foedera rumpat,*
> *Ex infinito ne causam causa sequatur,*
> *Libera per terras unde haec animantibus exstat*
> *Unde est haec, inquam, fatis avolsa potestas*
> *Per quam progredimur quo ducit quemque voluntas,*
> *Declinamus item motus nec tempore certo*
> *Nec regione loci certa, sed ubi ipsa tulit mens?*[1]

But on what ground does Lucretius assert his doctrine of free will? He makes his confident appeal to consciousness and experience. Free will is revealed first in initiating movement. The impulse for action comes from the heart, and successively spreads through the various members of the body, and of this Lucretius presents a very forcible illustration.

> *Nam dubio procul his rebus sua cuique voluntas*
> *Principium dat et hinc motus per membra rigantur.*
> *Nonne vides etiam patefactis tempore puncto*
> *Carceribus non posse tamen prorumpere equorum*
> *Vim cupidam tam de subito quam mens avet ipsa?*
> *Omnis enim totum per corpus materiai*
> *Copia conquiri debet, concita per artus*
> *Omnis ut studium mentis conixa sequatur;*
> *Ut videas initum motus a corde creari*
> *Ex animique voluntate id procedere primum,*
> *Inde dari porro per totum corpus et artus.*[2]

[1] II, 251-60.
[2] Ib., 261-71.

But free will is also apparent in resisting compulsory movement, which differs from voluntary action in that it results from a blow or impulse from without.

> *Nec similest ut cum impulsi procedimus ictu*
> *Viribus alterius magnis magnoque coactu;*
> *Nam tum materiem totius corporis omnem*
> *Perspicuumst nobis invitis ire rapique,*
> *Donec eam refrenavit per membra voluntas.*
> *Iamne vides igitur, quamquam vis extera multos*
> *Pellat et invitos cogat procedere saepe*
> *Praecipitesque rapi, tamen esse in pectore nostro*
> *Quiddam quod contra pugnare obstareque possit?*
> *Cuius ad arbitrium quoque copia materiai*
> *Cogitur interdum flecti per membra per artus*
> *. Et proiecta refrenatur retroque residit.*[1]

The conclusion derived from these considerations is that there must be, in addition to movement by weight or gravity, κατὰ στάθμην, and movement by blows, or external influence, κατὰ πληγήν, the *swerve*, which has already been described.

> *Quare in seminibus quoque idem fateare necessest,*
> *Esse aliam praeter plagas et pondera causam*
> *Motibus, unde haec est nobis innata potestas,*
> *De nilo quoniam fieri nil posse videmus.*
> *Pondus enim prohibet ne plagis omnia fiant*
> *Externa quasi vi; sed ne mens ipsa necessum*
> *Intestinum habeat cunctis in rebus agendis*
> *Et devicta quasi hoc cogatur ferre patique,*
> *Id facit exiguum clinamen principiorum*
> *Nec regione loci certa nec tempore certo.*[2]

Upon a recapitulation of this argument one finds that, while it is unsatisfactory, mainly because it is impossible to account for the operations of the intellect on a purely materialistic hypothesis, and while Lucretius in specifying three causes of movement confuses

---

[1] II, 272-83.
[2] II, 284-93.

thought, having first asserted that movement by collision results from the swerve and afterward having placed the swerve before us as a separate cause of movement, yet the reasoning, from his standpoint, is close and strong. It amounts to this: We are conscious of the power of the will to originate action, which, beginning at the center, extends under our personal direction through the whole physical frame. We are also conscious of the difference between voluntary action and necessary movement. When a body is moved by an external impulse, it moves all at once. And we easily discriminate between moving of our own volition and being forced to move. In the latter case we experience a feeling of resistance in our breast which impels us to withstand the energy applied to us. The atoms which compose body are subject to the same influences. There is the impulse of gravity, the impulse of external force, but there must be also in all atoms, and especially in those finer ones which form the mind, the power to vary at will from the line of perpendicular descent. This is inevitable, for if the soul has this power, as we know from experience it has, and the atoms which compose soul have it not, then the first principle of the atomistic philosophy— *ex nihilo nihil fit*—is outraged. There is no way, according to Lucretius, to explain the existence of free will in men—the highest result of the atomistic evolution—except by admitting that it is an active principle in original matter. And there is no satisfactory method of accounting for this inherent quality of the atoms except to acknowledge the *clinamen principiorum nec regione loci certa nec tempore certo.*[1]

An element of respect for Democritus enters into this discussion on the part of Lucretius, who wished to make as distinct as possible his divergence from the older philosopher, while he lingers over the subject to show that his conclusions have not been inconsiderately taken, and also that he may combat the Stoics.[2]

Other points of controversial contact between the Epicurean system and Democritus, as disclosed by the poem of Lucretius, seem of secondary importance, and yet are sufficiently characteristic to demand

---

[1] Masson, *Atomic Theory of Lucretius*, pp. 127, 28.
[2] Munro, II, p. 136.

DEMOCRITUS. 63

attention. Democritus, as we learn chiefly from Aristotle and Diogenes Laertius, held that the atoms are not only infinite in multitude, but also in the number of their shapes. The grounds of this opinion were that "there is no reason why one shape should belong to them more than to another;" that " only on this supposition can it be explained that things that are so infinitely diverse are subject to so many changes and appear so differently to different people."[1] Aristotle says:

Δημόκριτος δὲ καὶ Λεύκιππος ἐκ σωμάτων ἀδιαιρέτων τἆλλα συγκεῖσθαί φασι, ταῦτα δ᾽ ἄπειρα καὶ τὸ πλῆθος εἶναι καὶ τὰς μορφάς, αὐτὰ δὲ πρὸς αὐτὰ διαφέρειν τούτοις ἐξ ὧν εἰσι καὶ θέσει καὶ τάξει τούτων.[2]

Diogenes Laertius declares that Democritus believed—

καὶ τὰς ἀτόμους δὲ ἀπείρους εἶναι κατὰ μέγεθος καὶ πλῆθος.[3]

Against this doctrine Epicurus is emphatic. He says:

πρός τε τούτοις τὰ ἄτομα τῶν σωμάτων καὶ μεστά, ἐξ ὧν καὶ αἱ συγκρίσεις γίνονται καὶ εἰς ἃ διαλύονται, ἀπερίληπτά ἐστι ταῖς διαφοραῖς τῶν σχημάτων· οὐ γὰρ δυνατὸν γενέσθαι τὰς τοσαύτας διαφορὰς ἐκ τῶν αὐτῶν σχημάτων περιειλημμένων. καὶ καθ᾽ ἑκάστην δὲ σχημάτισιν ἁπλῶς ἄπειροί εἰσιν αἱ ὅμοιαι, ταῖς δὲ διαφοραῖς οὐχ ἁπλῶς ἄπειροι ἀλλὰ μόνον ἀπερίληπτοι.[4]

Lucretius adheres to his master in that he states and argues that the number of atoms is finite, but he does not, like Epicurus, admit that the number is incalculably great. He refrains from declaring whether it is small or large. But he adduces cogent reasons for his belief. In order to have an infinite number of shapes of atoms, it would be necessary to have atoms infinite in magnitude. For suppose an atom has a limited number of least parts; their permutations will only give a limited number of shapes. To secure an infinite number of shapes, therefore, it would be necessary to keep adding parts to infinity, and thus we should eventually have atoms of infinite size, which has been demonstrated to be an impossibility. Again, were the shapes of atoms infinite in number, there would be no limit to the beauty of color and sound, or to that which is offensive. But

---
[1] Zeller, *Pre-Socratic Philosophy*, II, p. 223.
[2] *Ib.*, p. 224, 1.
[3] IX, 44.
[4] *Diogenes Laertius*, X, 42.

we know there is a limit to all this, as also to the heat and cold of the year, summer's heat and winter's cold being two points between which various degrees of temperature proceed in their order.[1]

Lucretius mentions Democritus by name when he combats, as he feels compelled to do, this philosopher's theory of the formation of the soul; but, while he deprecates his doctrine, he alludes to its author in terms of compliment.

> *Illud in his rebus nequaquam sumere possis,*
> *Democriti quod sancta viri sententia ponit,*
> *Corporis atque animi primordia singula privis*
> *Adposita alterniis variare, ac nectere memlra.*[2]

To say that between every pair of atoms which compose the body there is a finer atom of the soul, is to Lucretius a wholly groundless statement. In his judgment the atoms of the body are many times as numerous as those of the soul, and therefore distributed at much wider intervals than Democritus supposed.

> *Nam cum multo sunt animae elementa minora*
> *Quam quibus e corpus nobis et viscera constant,*
> *Tum numero quoque concedunt et rara per artus*
> *Dissita sunt dumtaxat; ut hoc promittere possis,*
> *Cuantula prima queant nobis iniecta ciere,*
> *Corpora sensiferos motus in corpore, tanta*
> *Intervalla tenere exordia prima animai.*
> *Nam neque pulveris interdum sentimus adhaesum*
> *Corpore nec membris incussam sidere cretam,*
> *Nec nebulam noctu neque aranei tenvia fila*
> *Obvia sentimus, quando obretimur euntes,*
> *Nec supera caput eiusdem cecidisse vietam*
> *Vestem nec plumas avium papposque volantis*
> *Qui nimia levitate cadunt plerumque gravatim,*
> *Nec repentis itum cuiusviscumque animantis*
> *Sentimus nec priva pedum vestigia quaeque,*
> *Corpore quae in nostro culices et cetera ponunt.*

---

[1] II, 478-521.
[2] III, 370-3.

*Usque adeo prius est in nobis multa ciendum,
Quam primordia sentiscant concussa animai
Semina corporibus nostris inmixta per artus,
Et quam in his intervallis luditantia possint
Concursare coire et dissultare vicissim.*[1]

This point of difference between Epicurus and Democritus Munro declares we should never have known *but for this passage in Lucretius*, for in many particulars the two were in accord on the question of the constitution of the soul as well as other subjects connected with the atomistic philosophy.[2]

On the origin of verbal designations, the teaching of Epicurus and Lucretius seems to have been at variance with the doctrine of Democritus. In his letter to Herodotus Epicurus says:

τὰ ὀνόματα ἐξ ἀρχῆς μὴ θέσει γενέσθαι, ἀλλ' αὐτὰς τὰς φύσεις τῶν ἀνθρώπων καθ' ἕκαστα ἔθνη ἴδια πασχούσας πάθη καὶ ἴδια λαμβανούσας φαντάσματα ἰδίως τὸν ἀέρα ἐκπέμπειν στελλόμενον ὑφ' ἑκάστων τῶν παθῶν καὶ τῶν φαντασμάτων, ὡς ἄν ποτε καὶ ἡ παρὰ τοὺς τόπους τῶν ἐθνῶν διαφορὰ ᾖ· ὕστερον δὲ κοινῶς καθ' ἕκαστα ἔθνη τὰ ἴδια τεθῆναι πρὸς τὸ τὰς δηλώσεις ἧττον ἀμφιβόλους γενέσθαι ἀλλήλοις καὶ συντομωτέρως δηλουμένας κ.τ.λ.[3]

Terms of description and the language of common life were not directly imparted, but are the product of a necessary evolution. Nature and the multiplying needs of men prompted them to invent forms of speech. This is the conviction of Lucretius, who says:

*At varios linguae sonitus natura subegit
Mittere et utilitas expressit nomina rerum,
Non alia longe ratione atque ipsa videtur
Protrahere ad gestum pueros infantia linguae,
Cum facit ut digito quae sint praesentia monstrent.
Sentit enim vim quisque suam quoad possit abuti.*

All creatures feel their natural powers before these powers have been developed. The calf butts before his horns protrude; panthers and lions fight ere teeth and claws have appeared; and birds attempt flight before their pinnions have been fully plumed.

---

[1] III, 374-95.
[2] Munro, II, p. 194.
[3] *Diogenes Laertius*, X, 75, 76.

> *Proinde putare aliquem tum nomina distribuisse*
> *Rebus et inde homines didicisse vocabula prima,*
> *Desiperest.*

How could any one man know what he ought to teach, and how could he succeed in inducing other men to learn from him? And what hinders that man should apply different sounds to denote various things, when, as is well known, the brutes pursue this process; as for example, dogs, horses, sea-gulls, crows?

> *Ergo si varii sensus animalia cogunt,*
> *Muta tamen cum sint, varias emittere voces,*
> *Quanto mortalis magis accumst tum potuisse*
> *Dissimilis alia atque alia res voce notare!* [1]

Such is the reasoning of Lucretius, with which it is asserted Democritus did not agree.[2]

The presentation of a variety of reasons for the rising of the Nile, a choice of which the student of natural phenomena is entitled to make for himself, is very characteristic of the Epicurean method of dealing with physical facts, and also brings Lucretius into quasi conflict with Democritus, who according to Diodorus held a positive theory of the cause of this phenomenon, which is included among others asserted by Lucretius as possible.[3]

> *Fit quoque uti pluviae forsan magis ad caput ei*
> *Tempore eo fiant, quod etesia flabra aquilonum*
> *Nubila coniciunt in eas tunc omnia partis.*
> *Scilicet ad mediam regionem ciecta diei*
> *Cum convenerunt, ibi ad altos denique montis*
> *Contrusae nubes coguntur vique premuntur.*[4]

This explanation Lucretius gives no higher place than he assigns to the popular opinion, which Democritus intended to refute.

There is also an implied difference between Lucretius and Democ-

---

[1] V, 1028-90.
[2] Munro, II, p. 335.
[3] *Ib.*, p. 378.
[4] VI, 729-34.

ritus on the subject of the gods; for on this matter the poet has accurately represented Epicurus, who, according to Augustinus, is at issue with Democritus.

Quamquam Democritus etiam hoc distare in naturalibus quaestionibus ab Epicuro dicitur, quod iste sentit inesse concursioni atomorum vim quandam animalem et spiritalem ; qua vi eum credo et imagines ipsas divinitate praeditas dicere, non omnes omnium rerum, sed deorum; et principia mentis esse in universis, quibus divinitatem tribuit, et animantes imagines, quae vel prodesse nobis soleant vel nocere: Epicurus vero neque aliquid in principiis rerum ponit praeter atomos id est corpuscula quaedam tam minuta, ut etiam dividi nequeant neque sentiri aut visu aut tactu possint: quorum corpusculorum concursu fortuito et mundos innumerabiles et animantia et ipsas animas fieri dicit et deos, quos humana forma non in aliquo mundo sed extra mundos atque inter mundos constituit; et non vult omnino aliquid praeter corpora cogitare, quae tamen ut cogitet imagines dicit ab ipsis rebus, quas atomis formari putat, defluere atque in animum introire subtiliores quam sunt illae imagines quae ad oculos veniunt. nam et videndi causam hanc esse dicit, ingentes quasdam imagines ita ut universum mundum conplectantur extrinsecus.[1]

---

[1] Usener, p. 237.

II.

PHILOSOPHERS TOWARD WHOM LUCRETIUS IS HOSTILE.

If the criticisms of Lucretius upon those philosophers with whose theories he disagrees appear in some instances to be unduly severe, it must be remembered that in his master he had an example of merciless and caustic censure. The references of Epicurus to the exponents of other schools of philosophy not infrequently descend to scurrility. Contemptuous reflections upon Nausiphanes, Plato, Aristotle, Protagoras, Heraclitus and even Democritus have been attributed to him.

καὶ ἐν ταῖς ἑπτὰ καὶ τριάκοντα βίβλιοις ταῖς περὶ φύσεως τὰ πλεῖστα ταὐτά [τε] λέγειν καὶ ἀντιγράφειν ἐν αὐταῖς ἄλλοις τε καὶ Ναυσιφάνει [τὰ πλεῖστα], κα αὐτῇ λέξει φάσκειν οὕτως 'Αλλ' ἴτωσαν· εἶχε γὰρ ἐκεῖνος ὠδίνων τὴν ἀπὸ τοῦ στόματος καύχησιν τὴν σοφιστικήν, καθά περ καὶ ἄλλοι πολλοὶ τῶν ἀνδραπόδων. καὶ αὐτὸν 'Επίκουρον ἐν ταῖς ἐπιστολαῖς περὶ Ναυσιφάνους λέγειν Ταῦτα ἤγαγεν αὐτὸν εἰς ἔκστασιν τοιαύτην, ὥστε μοι λοιδορεῖσθαι καὶ ἀποκαλεῖν διδάσκαλον. πλεύμονά τε αὐτὸν ἐκάλει καὶ ἀγράμματον καὶ ἀπατεῶνα καὶ πόρνην· τούς τε περὶ Πλάτωνα Διονυσοκόλακας καὶ αὐτὸν Πλάτωνα χρυσοῦν, καὶ 'Αριστοτέλη ἄσωτον, (ὃν) καταφαγόντα τὴν πατρῴαν οὐσίαν στρατεύεσθαι καὶ φαρμακοπωλεῖν· φορμοφόρον τε Πρωταγόραν καὶ γραφέα Δημοκρίτου καὶ ἐν κώμαις γράμματα διδάσκειν· 'Ηράκλειτόν τε κυκητήν· καὶ Δημόκριτον Ληρόκριτον· καὶ 'Αντίδωρον Σαννίδωρον· τούς τε Κυνικοὺς ἐχθροὺς τῆς 'Ελλάδος· καὶ τοὺς διαλεκτικοὺς πολυφθόρους· Πύρρωνα δὲ ἀμαθῆ καὶ ἀπαίδευτον.[1]

The most notable thing in this passage, of course, is the fact that even Democritus, to whom Epicurus was so much indebted, comes in for his share of obloquy. Cicero confirms in a large degree the reports preserved by Diogenes Laertius.

Nam Phaedro nihil elegantius, nihil humanius; sed stomachabatur senex, si quid asperius dixeram, cum Epicurus Aristotelem vexarit contumeliosissime, Phaedoni Socratico turpissime male dixerit, Metrodori, sodalis sui, fratrem, Timocraten, quia nescio quid in philosophia dis-

---
[1] *Diogenes Laertius*, X. 7, 8.

sentiret, totis voluminibus conciderit, in Democritum ipsum, quem secutus est, fuerit ingratus, Nausiphanen, magistrum suum, a quo (non) nihil didicerat, tam male acceperit.[1]

With such traditions before him and filled with an idolatrous veneration for his master, it is not strange that Lucretius exhibited some severity in the treatment of his controversial antagonists, albeit his language is mild compared with that of Epicurus.

I. HERACLITUS.

Of the persons referred to by Lucretius in his poem, Heraclitus alone is severely denounced by name. It is interesting to note that this philosopher was himself abusive in his manner toward his competitors and contemporaries. Such honored names as Hesiod, Pythagoras, Xenophanes and Homer fell under the ban of his reprobation.

μεγαλόφρων δὲ γέγονε παρ' ὁντιναοῦν, καὶ ὑπερόπτης· ὡς καὶ ἐκ τοῦ συγγράμματος αὐτοῦ δῆλον, ἐν ᾧ φησι,Πολυμαθίη νόον οὐ διδάσκει. Ἡσίοδον γὰρ ἂν ἐδίδαξε καὶ Πυθαγόρην, αὖθίς τε Ξενοφάνεά τε καὶ Ἑκαταῖον. Εἶναι γὰρ ἓν τὸ σοφὸν ἐπίστασθαι γνώμην, ᾗτε οἱ ἐγκυβερνήσει πάντα διὰ πάντων. τὸν Ὅμηρον ἔφασκεν ἄξιον ἐκ τῶν ἀγώνων ἐκβάλλεσθαι καὶ ῥαπίζεσθαι, καὶ Ἀρχίλοχον ὁμοίως.[2]

At the same time, as has been pointed out by scholars, Heraclitus was influenced by some of the teachers whom he antagonized, notably by Xenophanes, with whose views of the heavenly bodies he undoubtedly sympathized.[3]

The avowed reason for the animosity of Lucretius toward Heraclitus, as exhibited in the passage now to be considered, is that he is the leader of those philosophers who assert that fire is the original essence from which everything has been derived. The Epicurean physics is arrayed against all systems that ascribe primordial matter to one, two or any limited number of substances. This of itself would be sufficient to bring the condemnation of Lucretius down

---
[1] *De Nat. Deor.*, I, 93.
[2] *Diogenes Laertius*, IX, 1.
[3] Ueberweg, *Hist. Phil.*, I, 39.

upon the head of Heraclitus. But when the element chosen to stand for all matter is fire, the whole Stoic school seems to be involved, and the virulence of the Epicurean poet is largely explained, as will become more apparent later by the deathless hostility existing between the "porch" and the "garden." It is a truly Epicurean and natural temper which displays itself in the lines with which Lucretius begins the attack upon Heraclitus.

> *Heraclitus init quorum dux proelia primus,*
> *Clarus ob obscuram linguam magis inter inanis*
> *Quamde gravis inter Graios qui vera requirunt.*
> *Omnia enim stolidi magis admirantur amantque,*
> *Inversis quae sub verbis latitantia cernunt,*
> *Veraque constituunt quae belle tangere possunt*
> *Auris et lepido quae sunt fucata sonore.*[1]

The taunt of obscurity contained in these lines originated as much from the reputation given Heraclitus by several writers of antiquity, as from any personal conviction which possessed Lucretius. The title ὁ σκοτεινός was early applied to Heraclitus.

ἄνδρες δ' ἀξιόλογοι γεγόνασιν ἐν αὐτῇ τῶν μὲν παλαιῶν Ἡράκλειτός τε ὁ σκοτεινὸς καλούμενος κ.τ.λ.[2]

The earliest employment of this term in connection with Heraclitus is said to be found in *Ps. Aristotle, De Mundo*, 5, unless this work is later than the time of Hannibal, in which case the passage in *Livy*, xxiii, 39, would indicate an earlier origin.[3]

The testimony of Cicero is to the same effect as that already given. *Heraclitus, cognomento qui σκοτεινός perhibetur, quia de natura nimis obscure memoravit.*[4]

Sed omnia vestri, Balbe, solent ad igneam vim referre Heraclitum, ut opinor, sequentes, quem ipsum non omnes interpretantur uno modo; qui quoniam quid diceret intelligi noluit, omittamus, etc.[5]

---

[1] I, 638-44.
[2] *Strabon*, XIV, 25 in Ritter et Preller, 22b.
[3] Munro, II, 84.
[4] *De Fin.*, II, 15.
[5] *De Nat. Deor.*, III, 35.

In a similar tenor is the witness of Diogenes Laertius.

ἀνέθηκε δ' αὐτὸ εἰς τὸ τῆς Ἀρτέμιδος ἱερόν, ὡς μέν τινες, ἐπιτηδεύσας ἀσαφέστερον γράψαι, ὅπως οἱ δυνάμενοι προσίοιεν αὐτῷ καὶ μὴ ἐκ τοῦ δημώδους εὐκαταφρόνητον εἴη. τοῦτον δὲ καὶ ὁ Τίμων ὑπογράφει, λέγων.
τοῖς δ' ἔνι κοκκυστὴς ὀχλολοίδορος Ἡράκλειτος
αἰνικτὴς ἀνόρουσε.[1]

In the letter from Darius, the son of Hystaspes, to Heraclitus we have further evidence of the recondite character of the Ephesian philosopher's writings.

τῶν δὲ πλείστων ἐποχὴν ἔχοντα· ὥστε καὶ τοὺς ἐπιπλεῖστον μετεσχηκότας συγγραμμάτων, διαπορεῖσθαι τῆς ὀρθῆς δοκούσης γεγράφθαι παρά σοι διηγήσεως.[2]

The saying that a Delian diver was required to fathom the depths of his composition has been attributed both to Socrates and to a certain Crates, who is reputed to be the first person who brought the work of Heraclitus into Central Greece.

A more favorable construction has, however, been placed upon the literary performances of Heraclitus by some authors, who declare in certain instances that his obscurity is due to the brevity with which he expresses himself. Others think that the figurative style of his speech has much to do with the difficulty of understanding him. Others attribute this fault to a certain loose method of expression; while the opinion is held in still other quarters that Heraclitus had no intention of explaining the matters which he proposed for consideration. *Huc accedit quod et omnis illorum temporum oratio philosophiae difficiles aditus praebebat et ille proponere malebat quae sentiret quam exponere.*[3]

On the other hand, it is asserted that he sometimes wrote with lucidity and brilliancy.

λαμπρῶς τε ἐνίοτε ἐν τῷ συγγράμματι καὶ σαφῶς ἐκβάλλει, ὥστε καὶ τὸν νωθέστατον ῥᾳδίως γνῶναι καὶ διαρμα ψυχῆς λαβεῖν· ἡ βραχύτης καὶ τὸ βάρος τῆς ἑρμηνείας ἀσύγκριτον.[4]

---

[1] *Diog. Laer.*, IX, 6.
[2] *Ib.*, IX, 13.
[3] Ritter et Preller, 23*a*
[4] *Diog. Laer.*, IX, 7.

He himself compared his gravity with the seriousness of oracles when correctly interpreted.

ὁ ἄναξ (οὗ τὸ μαντεῖόν ἐστι τὸ) ἐν Δελφοῖς οὔτε λέγει οὔτε κρύπτει, ἀλλὰ σημαίνει. σίβυλλα δὲ μαινομένῳ στόματι ἀγέλαστα καὶ ἀκαλλώπιστα καὶ ἀμύριστα φθεγγομένη χιλίων ἐτέων ἐξικνέεται τῇ φωνῇ διὰ τὸν θεόν.[1]

There are a few persons who doubtless will agree with Prof. Ferrier that Heraclitus is "the deepest probably, if also the darkest, of all the thinkers of antiquity."[2]

The argument of Lucretius against Heraclitus betrays perhaps more clearly than any other controversial passage in his poem how difficult it is for him to argue from any standpoint except his own. His reasoning is neither as cogent nor as fair in this instance as in some other portions of his work. Accepting his own premises and proceeding from his own point of view, his argument is weighty enough; but there are evidences of either a wilful attempt to misrepresent the opinions of Heraclitus, or a disposition to allow the prejudices of his school against the Stoics, with whom he identifies Heraclitus, to obscure the real teaching of the Ephesian. On the supposition that the fire out of which the universe is evolved according to Heraclitus is the same as the fire which he pictures to his own consciousness, Lucretius presents his objections in this order:

1. It is impossible to obtain such a variety of things from fire.

2. Condensation and rarefaction are insufficient to account for this variety, because they effect no qualitative change.

3. Heraclitus denies void in things, without which condensation and rarefaction are inconceivable.

4. When he declares that changes occur by the extinction of the fire he is at fault, for that would mean annihilation, and things would then need to be produced from nothing, which is contrary to the first principle of true philosophy.

5. To assert that fire is the only real existence, all other things being only apparent is to deny the infallibility of the senses, a fundamental doctrine of Epicureanism.[3]

---

[1] Fr. 11, 12, in Fairbanks, *First Philosophers of Greece*, p. 26.
[2] Masson, *Atomic Theory of Lucretius*, p. 27, 3.
[3] I, 645-764.

The question suggested by an examination of the argument thus outlined is: To what extent does Lucretius represent the actual position of Heraclitus? What, for example, is the precise significance of the fire which the latter employs to indicate primitive matter? That Heraclitus has adopted fire as the primordial sole element from which all things have been derived, is certified in the most unequivocal manner.

ἐκ πυρὸς τὰ πάντα συνεστάναι, καὶ εἰς τοῦτο ἀναλύεσθαι... πῦρ εἶναι στοιχεῖον, καὶ πυρὸς ἀμοιβὴν τὰ πάντα ἀραιώσει καὶ πυκνώσει τὰ γινόμενα... καὶ ἕνα εἶναι κόσμον. γεννᾶσθαί τε αὐτὸν ἐκ πυρός, καὶ πάλιν ἐκπυροῦσθαι κατά τινας... πυκνούμενον γὰρ τὸ πῦρ ἐξυγραίνεσθαι, συνιστάμενόν τε γίνεσθαι ὕδωρ· πηγνύμενον δὲ τὸ ὕδωρ, εἰς γῆν τρέπεσθαι· καὶ ταύτην ὁδὸν ἐπὶ τὸ κάτω εἶναι. πάλιν τε αὐτὴν τὴν γῆν χεῖσθαι, ἐξ ἧς τὸ ὕδωρ γίνεσθαι· ἐκ δὲ τούτου τὰ λοιπὰ σχεδὸν πάντα, ἐπὶ τὴν ἀναθυμίασιν ἀνάγων τὴν ἀπὸ τῆς θαλάττης. αὕτη δέ ἐστιν ἡ ἐπὶ τὸ ἄνω ὁδός.[1]

But was the fire of Heraclitus that of Lucretius? The poet would have us think so, and the words of Cicero already cited seem to claim as much. Lucretius apparently has before his mind constantly the visible flame, the process of combustion, and other phenomena which appeal to the senses. But no student of the fragments of Heraclitus can be persuaded that he was tied to any such narrow conceptions. Grote admits that the Lucretian interpretation is countenanced by some striking passages from Heraclitus, but maintains that from the whole mass of his works, in as far as we possess them, "it appears that his main doctrine was not physical but metaphysical or ontological; that the want of general adequate terms induced him to clothe it in a multitude of symbolical illustrations, among which fire was only one, though the most prominent and significant."[2] The latter part of this statement would seem to be scarcely accurate, since Heraclitus evidently regarded fire, not simply as one of several symbols which could serve as illustrations of his doctrine, but as the one inclusive symbol, which in a special sense answered the requirements of ever-changing nature. With this modification Zeller would be in substantial harmony with Grote's view. The former says in effect, that with the doctrine that all things are in constant flux as the

---

[1] *Diogenes Laertius*, IX. 7, 8, 9. Ἡράκλειτός φησιν ἅπαντα γίνεσθαί ποτε πῦρ. Aristotle, *Phys.* III, 5, 205a, 3. Ritter et Preller, 29a.
[2] Grote, *Plato*, I, 27.

fundamental principle of his philosophy, fire seems to Heraclitus to be the living, moving element in nature. The foundation of this theory, lies in the fact that fire seems to the philosopher to be the substance which least of all has a permanent consistency or allows it in another; and he consequently understands by his fire not merely flame, but warmth in general, for which reason he also designates it as vapor or breath—ψυχή. His reason for adopting fire as the material of the universe was "in order to express the absolute life of nature, and to make the restless alternation of phenomena comprehensible. Fire is not to him an unvarying substance out of which things derived were compounded, but which in this union remains qualitatively unchanged, like the elements of Empedocles or the primitive substances of Anaxagoras; "it is the essence which ceaselessly passes into all elements, the universal nourishing matter which, in its eternal circulation, permeates all parts of the cosmos, assumes in each a different constitution, produces individual existences, and again resolves itself; and by its absolute motion causes the restless beating of the pulse of nature.[1]

Heraclitus has left a statement which harmonizes with this phraseology, and serves to elucidate his meaning in the use of fire:

πυρὸς ἀνταμείβεται πάντα καὶ πῦρ ἁπάντων, ὥσπερ χρυσοῦ χρήματα καὶ χρημάτων χυσός.[2]

Brandis, commenting upon this, as quoted by Munro,[3] says that fire "is that for which all things are exchanged as wares for gold; but it changes itself as little into the things, as gold changes into these wares." But Zeller[4] puts a somewhat different construction on the passage when he says: "Herein he gives us to understand that the derived arises out of the primitive matter, not merely by combination and separation, but by transformation, by qualitative change; for in the barter of wares for gold, the substance does not remain, but only the worth of it."

Another pertinent inquiry in this connection is this: Does Lucretius correctly represent Heraclitus in attributing to him the hypothesis

---

[1] Zeller, *Pre-Socratic Philosophy*, II, 23.
[2] Fr., 22, in Fairbanks, *First Phil. Greece*, p. 30.
[3] II, 85.
[4] *Pre-Socratic Philosophy*, II, 28.

of condensation and rarefaction to account for the derivation of things? There is undoubtedly on the surface of much that is credited to Heraclitus an indication of this theory. The passage already quoted from Diogenes Laertius [1] certainly bears this construction. Other testimony is equally direct and definite.

Ἡράκλειτος . . . ἀρχὴν τῶν ὅλων τὸ πῦρ . . τούτου δὲ κατασβεννυμένου κοσμοποιεῖσθαι τὰ πάντα. πρῶτον μὲν γὰρ τὸ παχυμερέστατον αὐτοῦ εἰς αὑτὸ συστελλόμενον γῆν γίνεσθαι, ἔπειτα ἀναχαλωμένην τὴν γῆν ὑπὸ τοῦ πυρὸς φύσει ὕδωρ ἀποτελεῖσθαι, ἀναθυμιώμενον δὲ ἀέρα γίνεσθαι.[2]

Ἵππασος καὶ Ἡράκλειτος ἓν καὶ οὗτοι καὶ κινούμενον καὶ πεπερασμένον, ἀλλὰ πῦρ ἐποίησαν τὴν ἀρχὴν καὶ ἐκ πυρὸς ποιοῦσι τὰ ὄντα πυκνώσει καὶ μανώσει καὶ διαλύουσι πάλιν εἰς πῦρ ὡς ταύτης μιᾶς οὔσης φύσεως τῆς ὑποκειμένης· πυρὸς γὰρ ἀμοιβὴν εἶναί φησιν Ἡράκλειτος πάντα.[3]

But this interpretation of Heraclitus, which is made by later writers exclusively, is irreconcilable with the fundamental principle of his philosophy, which is that all things are in perpetual flux—there is nothing permanent. It is inevitable that when fire passes into moisture and thence into earth, condensation occurs, and when this process is reversed, rarefaction just as certainly takes place. But these are results, and not causes of a change of substance. The phraseology employed by Heraclitus is foreign to the notion of condensation and rarefaction, and combination and separation of substances. His terms are *transmutation*, *kindling* and *extinguishing*, *life* and *death*. Moreover, the idea of one immutable primitive substance is utterly incongruous with the underlying principle of his philosophy. Though fire was in his view the essence from which all things were evolved, it was not so in the sense in which Thales or Anaximenes made water or rain the original element. The early physicists regarded their elements as abiding without change in the midst of the constant mutations of things derived. The fire of Heraclitus, on the other hand, is that element which by its perpetual transmutation effects these changes.[4]

But Lucretius contends that without void in matter, the existence

---
[1] IX, 8, 9.
[2] *Plutarch, Plac.*, I, 3, 25, in Zeller. *Pre-Socratic Philosophy.* II. 28, 2.
[3] *Simplicius, Phys.*, 6r, 23, 33D in Ritter et Preller, 29c.
[4] Zeller, *Pre-Soc. Phil.*, II, 28-30.

of which Heraclitus denies, there could be no such processes as rarefaction and condensation; and hence, even if they were sufficient to account for the variety in nature produced from fire as the sole original element, on his opponent's own theory, they are not to be considered.

> *Id quoque, si faciant admixtum rebus inane,*
> *Denseri poterunt ignes rarique relinqui.*
> *Sed quia multa sibi cernunt contraria nasci*
> *Et fugitant in rebus inane relinquere purum,*
> *Ardua dum metuunt, amittunt vera viai,*
> *Nec rursum cernunt exempto rebus inani*
> *Omnia denseri fierique ex omnibus unum*
> *Corpus, nil ab se quod possit mittere raptim;*
> *Aestifer ignis uti lumen iacit atque vaporem,*
> *Ut videas non e stipatis partibus esse.*[1]

Again, bearing in mind the terminology of Heraclitus referred to above, which apparently involves the ideas of death and extinction, Lucretius fancies he has hit upon an argument calculated utterly to destroy his adversary, when he declares that the extinguishing of the primordial fire to produce the changes of nature would signify that things were constantly being produced out of nothing, which is contrary to the first principle of rational philosophy.

> *Quod si forte alia credunt ratione potesse*
> *Ignis in coetu stingui mutareque corpus,*
> *Scilicet ex nulla facere id si parte reparcent,*
> *Occidet ad nilum nimirum funditus ardor*
> *Omnis et e nilo fient quaecumque creantur.*[2]

But when Heraclitus conceives of his fire as extinguished, it is certainly not in the sense in which Lucretius fancies he does, for he plainly declares that his fire is never destroyed. The lightning flash passes away, but the essential warmth is still in existence. The sun goes down and darkness follows, but Helios is not quenched. The

---

[1] I, 655-64.
[2] I 665-69.

fire of Heraclitus "is not like sunlight, connected with a particular and therefore changing phenomenon, but is the universal essence, which is contained in all things as their substance."[1] The remarkable approach which Heraclitus thus makes to the nebular hypothesis of modern science imparts to his doctrines an exceedingly vital interest.

An examination of the Heraclitean doctrine of the senses, suggested by the criticism of Lucretius, presents another difficulty of interpretation. Had Lucretius some better knowledge of the opinions of Heraclitus than we possess in order to enable him to make the assertions regarding his views contained in the following lines? is a problem propounded by Munro:[2]

> *Dicere porro ignem res omnis esse neque ullam*
> *Rem veram in numero rerum constare nisi ignem,*
> *Quod facit hic idem, perdelirum esse videtur.*
> *Nam contra sensus ab sensibus ipse repugnat*
> *Et labefactat eos unde omnia credita pendent,*
> *Unde hic cognitus est ipsi quem nominat ignem;*
> *Credit enim sensus ignem cognoscere vere,*
> *Cetera non credit, quae nilo clara minus sunt.*[3]

There can be no doubt that Heraclitus did distrust the senses.

κακοὶ μάρτυρες ἀνθρώποισι ὀφθαλμοὶ καὶ ὦτα, βαρβάρους ψυχὰς ἐχόντων.[4]
τήν τε οἴησιν, ἱερὰν νόσον ἔλεγε· καὶ τὴν ὅρασιν, ψεύδεσθαι.[5]

According to his opinion "what our senses perceive is merely the fleeting phenomenon, not the essence."[6] Fire alone reveals original matter. Other things which appeal to our senses actually conceal, instead of disclosing, the essential quality of matter. Separate phenomena at best can only afford us a meagre and fractional view of that universal nature which is in constant flux. The testimony of the senses is, therefore, never true, for the reason that it is always fragmentary and inexact. The unwisdom of the generality of mankind

---

[1] Zeller *Pre-Soc. Phil.*, II, 26.
[2] II, 88.
[3] I, 690-97.
[4] *Heracl.*, Fr., 4, in Fairbanks, *First Phil. Greece*, p. 24.
[5] *Diogenes Laertius*, IX, 7.
[6] Zeller, *Pre-Socratic Philosophy*, II, 88.

is consequently seen in the fact that the mass depend for knowledge upon the evidence of the senses, an opinion with which Lucretius is wholly at variance, being fully persuaded in his own mind of the infallability of the sense perceptions.

> *Quod mihi cum vanum tum delirum esse videtur;*
> *Quo referemus enim? quid nobis certius ipsis*
> *Sensibus esse potest, qui vera ac falsa notemus?*[1]

After his treatment of Empedocles and his four elements, in which fire is included, Lucretius apparently swings back to Heraclitus, though there is a difference among critics as to whether he actually refers to the Ephesian philosopher in the passage we are about to consider.[2] Munro thinks that Lucretius may be "viewing Heraclitus through the glosses of the Stoics," and may be "thinking among other theories of his όδὸς ἄνω κάτω;" but, as he affirms, no scholar would attribute to him the interchange of the *four* elements.[3] Hallier, on the other hand, whose contribution to the literature on Empedocles and Lucretius has already been noted, believes that this passage points directly to Heraclitus, and not to the Stoics at all, except (perhaps he would admit) in a remote and adapted sense. After quoting the citation on the doctrines of Heraclitus from *Diogenes Laertius*, IX, 9, which we have given above (p. 73), and which he declares to be almost identical in language with *Lucretius*, I, 782-88, he says: *Unde aliquantum discrepant quae de Stoicis refert Diogenes Laertius, VII, 142,*[4] which runs as follows:

γίνεσθαι δὲ τὸν κόσμον, ὅταν ἐκ πυρὸς ἡ οὐσία τραπῇ δι' ἀέρος εἰς ὑγρόν, εἶτα τὸ παχυμερὲς αὐτοῦ συστὰν ἀποτελεσθῇ γῆ, τὸ δὲ λεπτομερὲς ἐξαραιωθῇ καὶ τοῦτ' ἐπὶ πλέον λεπτυνθὲν πῦρ ἀπογεννήσῃ· εἶτα κατὰ μίξιν ἐκ τούτων φυτά τε καὶ ζῷα καὶ τὰ ἄλλα γένη.

The opposition of Lucretius to the doctrine of transmutation, contained in the passage under discussion, is that primordia cannot thus change, but must be distinct and unchangeable, otherwise they would be annihilated; for, according to his view, whenever a thing changes and deserts its own limitations, immediately the death of

---

[1] I, 698-700.
[2] I, 782-802.
[3] Munro, II, 95.
[4] *Lucreti Carmina e Fragmentis Empedoclis Adumbrata*, p. 20.

that which was ensues. Hence, if the elements, which the philosophers under consideration have described, are not formed out of things themselves immutable, we should have things returning to nothing, and again defy the first principle of all true philosophy.

> *Quin potius tali natura praedita quaedam*
> *Corpora constituas, ignem si forte crearint,*
> *Posse eadem demptis paucis paucisque tributis,*
> *Ordine mutato et motu, facere aeris auras.*
> *Sic alias aliis rebus mutarier omnis?*[1]—

exclaims Lucretius, who in this as all other instances, argues from his own standpoint exclusively.

It may serve to mitigate in our judgment the severity of Lucretius' assault upon Heraclitus to remember that he is principally actuated by his hostility to the Stoics, who adopted very largely the physical theory of the origin of the universe taught by Heraclitus, as the Epicureans employed that of Leucippus and Democritus for their purpose. Munro feels that the use of plural subjects and verbs in the section under survey (I, 645–89), undoubtedly points to the Stoic school.[2]

2. THE STOICS.

The antagonism of Lucretius toward the Stoic school was one of the inevitable consequences of his absolute confidence in Epicurus. Trusting him with unquestioning devotion, he could not avoid being intolerant of that system of philosophy which, at the time he wrote, was the only successful rival of Epicureanism. Though Lucretius never mentions the Stoics or their chief teachers, Zeno, Chrysippus and Cleanthes by name, there are repeated allusions to them in his verses, which betray an intensity of feeling not always manifest in other polemical passages. Twice in Book I (641, 1068)· he contemptuously calls the Stoics *stolidi*, a word containing more bitterness

---
[1] I, 798 802.
[2] Munro, II. p. 83.

than he evinces in the case of any other school. This hostility of Lucretius to the philosophers of the "porch," one might almost call an inherited passion. Reference has already been made to the unfriendliness with which Epicurus spoke of competitors for philosophic honors.[1] Diogenes Laertius endeavors to refute these reports of harshness on the part of Epicurus toward his rivals, insisting that they are calumnies, and citing evidences of his kindness and affability.

μεμήνασι δ' οὗτοι. τῷ γὰρ ἀνδρὶ μάρτυρες ἱκανοὶ τῆς ἀνυπερβλήτου πρὸς πάντας εὐγνωμοσύνης ἥ τε πατρὶς χαλκαῖς εἰκόσι τιμήσασα, οἵ τε φίλοι τοσοῦτοι τὸ πλῆθος ὡς μηδ' ἂν πόλεσιν ὅλαις μετρεῖσθαι δύνασθαι, οἵ τε γνώριμοι πάντες ταῖς δογματικαῖς αὐτοῦ σειρῆσι προσκατασχεθέντες πλὴν Μητροδώρου τοῦ Στρατονικέως πρὸς Καρνεάδην ἀποχωρήσαντος, τάχα βαρυνθέντος ταῖς ἀνυπερβλήτοις αὐτοῦ χρηστότησιν . . ἥ τε πρὸς τοὺς γονέας εὐχαριστία, καὶ ἡ πρὸς τοὺς ἀδελφοὺς εὐποιΐα, πρός τε τοὺς οἰκέτας ἡμερότης, . . καθόλου τε ἡ πρὸς πάντας αὐτοῦ φιλανθρωπία. τῆς μὲν γὰρ πρὸς θεοὺς ὁσιότητος καὶ πρὸς πατρίδα φιλίας ἄλεκτος ἡ διάθεσις.[2]

But an attitude of friendliness toward disciples and admirers is certainly not inconsistent with injustice and hatred toward philosophic opponents. Moreover, the defence which Diogenes Laertius makes is not wholly disinterested, since if not a disciple himself, he was at least a warm friend of the Epicureans.[3] The spirit of hostility which Epicurus exhibited toward the champions of other philosophic schemes he transmitted to his followers, whose most conspicuous characteristic, as we have seen, was their servile devotion to their master's instruction. It was natural that a contention which had ensued for two hundred years should suffer no diminution with the lapse of time. In agreement with this probability we find Zeno, the Sidonian, a σχολάρχης, who wrote in the time of Lucretius, indulging in positive scurrility when he mentions the older philosoophers as well as his contemporaries. Cicero[4] declares: *Zeno quidem non eos solum, qui tum erant, Apollodorum, Silum, ceteros, figebat maledictis, sed Socraten ipsum, parentem philosophiae, Latino verbo utens*

---

[1] *Diogenes Laertius*, X, 7, 8.
[2] *Ib.*, X, 9.
[3] Zeller, *Stoics, Epicureans and Sceptics* (Eng. Tr.), p. 416, 1.
[4] *De Nat. Deor.*, I, 93.

scurram Atticum fuisse dicebat Chrysippum nemquam nisi Chrysippam.[1] *vocebat.* Such contumelious treatment was sure to be resented. The Stoics of earlier days did not hesitate to heap the foulest abuse upon Epicurus[2] in return for his strictures upon their philosophy; and their successors were not slow to emulate them in this respect when they came to consider the later Epicureans. But the Stoic charges of gross immorality have never been proven against Epicurus and his immediate disciples. It is very natural that a company of persons who assert that pleasure is the highest good should be open to the suspicion of sensuality. And this likelihood was increased in the case of Epicurus by the admission of women, some of whom were of easy virtue, to the garden where his philosophy was taught. Such conduct, however, was not extraordinary in the state of Greek society at that time. And in all justice it must be confessed that the idolatrous veneration of his adherents for Epicurus is difficult of explanation on the supposition that he was a man of impure character. Moreover, his letters here and there give evidence of a righteousness almost Puritanic in some particulars. That he subsisted on frugal fare, and refrained from excesses of every sort, is the testimony not only of his friends,[3] but also of those who ridiculed his abstemiousness.[4] Great writers subsequent to Lucretius, such as Seneca, Juvenal and Lucian, vindicate the name of Epicurus from the dishonor

---

[1] Or, *Chesippum.*

[2] Διότιμος δ ὁ Στωικὸς δυσμενῶς ἔχων πρὸς αὐτὸν πικρότατα αὐτὸν διαβέβληκεν, ἐπιστολὰς φέρων πεντήκοντα ἀσελγεῖς ὡς 'Επικούρου· καὶ ὁ τὰ εἰς Χρύσιππον ἀναφερόμενα ἐπιστόλια ὡς 'Επικούρου συντάξας. ἀλλὰ καὶ οἱ περὶ Ποσειδώνιον τὸν Στωικὸν καὶ Νικόλαος καὶ Σωτίων - - καὶ Διονύσιος ὁ 'Αλικαρνασσεύς. - - καὶ Λεοντίῳ συνεῖναι τῇ ἑταίρᾳ· - - καὶ ἄλλαις δὲ πολλαῖς ἑταίραις γράφειν, καὶ μάλιστα Λεοντίῳ ἧς καὶ Μητρόδωρον ἐρασθῆναι. - - 'Επίκτητός τε κιναιδολόγον αὐτὸν καλεῖ καὶ τὰ μάλιστα λοιδορεῖ. καὶ μὴν καὶ Τιμοκράτης - - φησὶ δὶς αὐτὸν τῆς ἡμέρας ἐμεῖν ἀπὸ τρυφῆς. - - συνεῖναί τε αὐτῷ τε καὶ Μητροδώρῳ ἑταίρας καὶ ἄλλας, Μαμμάριον καὶ 'Ηδεῖαν καὶ 'Ερώτιον καὶ Νικίδιον.—*Diog. Laer.,* X, 3-7. Usener, *Epicurea,* pp. 360-2.

[3] Διοκλῆς δὲ ἐν τῇ τρίτῃ τῆς ἐπιδρομῆς φησιν - εὐτελέστατα καὶ λιτότατα διαιτώμενοι· κοτύλῃ γοῦν, φησίν, οἰδινίου ἠρκοῦντο· τὸ δὲ πᾶν ὕδωρ ἦν αὐτοῖς ποτόν. πέμψον μοι τυροῦ φησὶ κυθριδίου, ἵν' ὅταν βούλωμαι πολυτελεύσασθαι δύνωμαι. *Ib.,* X. x. 11. *Cf.,* 130 144, 146.

[4] James Baldwin Brown. *Stoics and Saints,* p. 17 (Mac Millan & Co.).

which is attached to it through the perversion of his doctrines.[1] At the same time it must be confessed that there is nothing in his principles or system of philosophy to restrain those who espouse his teaching from a life of self-indulgence. That a convivialist will adopt such a scheme of doctrines to justify lascivious and effeminate conduct, is not only a natural inference, but a fact of history.

Usener, speaking of the opponents of the Epicureans, refers to the never-ending hostility of the Stoics in the following language:

Omnium longe acerbissimi et gravissimi Stoici. Quorum sectae cum a principio Epicuri philosophia omnis repugnaret, etiam magis contraria facta est, postquam Persaeus unam Stoicorum doctrinam servando regno et civitati utilem esse Antigono regi persuasit et ad regni commoda philosophiam revocavit. Prodiit Cleanthes adversarius ut Aristarchus Samius expertus est, acer vehemensque, qui non solum atomos inpugnaret sed etiam imaginem vividam exornando Virtutum ancillantium miserationem, odium Voluptatis dominantis commoveret. Iam magis magisque coeptum est odiis irisque dimicari. Ad infamandum Epicurum fuere qui epistulas inpudicas tamquam ab illo scriptas publicarent. Severissima plebiscita in Epicureos a Messeniis Lyctiis Phalannaeis facta multitudinis superstitiosae odio Stoicorum calumniis excitato.[2]

The Epicureans on their part were, of course, no less bitter in their criticisms upon the followers of Zeno. Philodemus, a close contemporary of Lucretius, brings serious charges of impiety against the Stoics. From the *Volumina Herculanensia* Usener makes this extract:

πάντες οὖν οἱ ἀπὸ Ζ(ή)νωνος εἰ καὶ ἀπέλ(ει)πον τὸ δαιμόνιον, ὥσπ(ε)ρ οἱ μὲν οὐκ ἀπ(έ)λειπον, (οἳ) δ' ἐν τισὶν οὐκ ἀπέ(λει)πον, ἵνα (θε)ὸν λέγου(σι)ν εἶναι, γίνεσθαι (δὲ) καὶ τὸ πᾶν σὺν τῆι ψυχῆι, πλανῶσιν δ' (ὡς) πολλοὺς ἀπολ(ε)ίπον(τες). ὥστ' (οὐ κα)τὰ ν(ό)μ(ο)ν θ(εοὺ)ς ἐννο)εῖν ἀ(λλ' ἀ)ναιρεῖν ἐπιδεικ(ν)ύσθωσαν τοῖς πολλοῖς, ἵνα μόνον ἅπαντα λέγοντες, οὐ πολλούς, οὐδὲ πάντας ὅσους ἡ κοινὴ (φ)ήμη παραδέδωκεν, ἡμῶν οὐ μόνον ὅσους φασὶν οἱ Πανέλληνες ἀλλὰ καὶ πλείονας εἶναι λεγόντων.[3]

---

[1] Sellar, *Roman Poets of the Republic*, p. 299. Seneca, *Vit. Be.*, 13, 1. *Ep.* 33, 2. Cf., *Cic. Fin.*, II, 25. 81. Zeller, *Stoics, Epicureans and Sceptics*, p. 487, 3.
[2] *Epicurea, Prefatio, LXXI. LXXII.*
[3] περὶ εὐσεβείας, in *Epicurea, Praefatio. LXXIII.*

Cicero refers to the master of the Epicurean school as *Epicurum, quem hebetem et rudem dicere solent Stoici*.[1] Knowing the animosity of some of the belligerents in the contests of the Stoics and the Epicureans, we easily conjecture the manner in which those treated one another, of whom we have no accurate record. Formerly, we are told,[2] there were extant many volumes of the controversial writings of Chrysippus bearing upon Epicurus, but we have now only an imperfect, though valuable, index of the productions of the famous Stoic, those treating of Epicurean tenets being as follows:

περὶ τοῦ καλοῦ καὶ τῆς ἡδονῆς, ἀποδείξεις πρὸς τὸ μὴ εἶναι τὴν ἡδονὴν τέλος, ἀποδείξεις πρὸς τὸ μὴ εἶναι τὴν ἡδονὴν ἀγαθόν.[3]

The hostility of Lucretius toward Stoicism, however, cannot be adequately accounted for on the mere ground of the traditional enmity existing between the two schools. Not only do irreconcilable differences occur immediately the systems are brought to the solution of the same fundamental problems, but there are remarkable points of agreement between them, which alone would be sufficient to beget an ungenerous rivalry. Epicureans and Stoics alike were in quest of the same *desideratum*—rest of soul (ἀταραξία). They both employed in this pursuit a philosophy thoroughly materialistic, and assigned to practical questions a supremacy over matters of pure speculation. The perceptions of the senses were by both regarded as the only standard by which truth could be measured. They were both agreed that accurate knowledge is attainable, otherwise there could be no positive action. Even in the consideration of the *summum bonum*, where it would be natural to expect the widest breach, it has been shown that the grounds of contentment and spiritual repose in both were exceedingly similar.[4] It has been truthfully asserted "that the

---

[1] *De Divinatione*, II, 50, 103.
[2] Usener, *Epicurea Praefatio, LXXIII*.
[3] *Diogenes Laertius*, VII, 202.
[4] "According to Zeno virtue, according to Epicurus pleasure, is the highest and only good; but the former in making virtue consist essentially in withdrawal from the senses or insensibility; the latter in seeking pleasure in repose of mind or inperturbability, are expressing the same belief. Man can only find unconditional and enduring satisfaction, when by means of knowledge he attains to a condition

tones of Lucretius might in many places be mistaken for those of a Stoic, rather than an Epicurean. In their resistance to the common forms of evil these systems were at one. Perhaps, too, in the positive good at which he aimed, the spirit of Lucretius was more that of a Stoic than he imagined."[1] Furthermore, both Epicureans and Stoics are devoid of any permanent interest in social life, and both would divorce the wise man from public and political activity. The very likeness[2] of these several approaches to the main question at issue was calculated to engender enmity and rancour. In addition to which there was an irrepressible conflict between the two schools in the detailed development of their materialistic views. Speaking broadly, the occasions of this contention may be best described in the language of another: "These divergencies appear particularly on the subject of nature, the Stoic regarding nature as a system of design, the Epicureans explaining it as a mechanical product. Whilst the Stoics adhered to fatalism, and saw God everywhere, the Epicureans held the theory of atoms and the theory of necessity. Whilst the Stoics were speculatively orthodox, the Epicureans were irreligious free-thinkers."[3] Hence it was inevitable that the author of *De Rerum Natura* should give large place to controversy with his master's chief antagonists.

Particular instances of conflict between Lucretius and the Stoic school appear early in the poem. The passage in which properties and accidents (*eventa et conjuncta*) are discussed[4] is directly opposed to the teaching of the rival philosophy which regards all states, qualities, virtues, emotions, etc., as corporeal.

---

of mind at rest with itself, and also to an independence of external attractions and misfortunes. . . . Neither the Stoic can separate happiness from virtue, nor the Epicurean separate virtue from happiness."—Zeller, *Stoics, Epicureans and Sceptics*, pp. 505, 6.

[1] Sellar, *Roman Poets of the Republic*, p. 363.

[2] "The united weight of all these points of resemblance is sufficient to warrant the assertion that, notwithstanding their difference, the Stoics and Epicureans stand on the same footing, and that the sharpness of contrast between them is owing to their laying hold of opposite sides of one and the same principle." Zeller, *Stoics, Epicureans and Sceptics*, p. 506.

[3] *Ib.*, p. 505.

[4] I, 430–82.

The Stoics and Epicureans were agreed that reality could only be ascribed to material objects. They argued in almost identical terms that whatever affects anything, or is in turn affected by anything, is bodily substance. Cicero[1] says: *Discrepabat etiam ab iisdem (superioribus Zeno), quod nullo modo arbitrabatur quidquam effici posse ab ea (natura), quae expers esset corporis—nec vero aut quod efficeret aliquid aut quod efficeretur posse esse non corpus.* Plutarch says: ὄντα γὰρ μόνα τὰ σώματα καλοῦσιν, ἐπειδὴ ὄντος τὸ ποιεῖν τε καὶ πάσχειν.[2]
With this declaration Epicurus concurs:

καθ' ἑαυτὸ δὲ οὐκ ἔστι νοῆσαι τὸ ἀσώματον πλὴν τοῦ κενοῦ. τὸ δὲ κενὸν οὔτε ποιῆσαι οὔτε παθεῖν δύναται, ἀλλὰ κίνησιν μόνον δι' ἑαυτοῦ τοῖς σώμασι παρέχεται.[3]

Lucretius says:

> *Praeterea per se quodcumque erit, aut faciet quid*
> *Aut aliis fungi debebit agentibus ipsum*
> *Aut erit, ut possunt in eo res esse gerique.*
> *At facere et fungi sine corpore nulla potest res*
> *Nec praebere locum porro nisi inane vacansque.*
> *Ergo praeter inane et corpora tertia per se*
> *Nulla potest rerum in numero natura relinqui,*
> *Nec quae sub sensus cadat ullo tempore nostros*
> *Nec ratione animi quam quisquam possit apisci.*[4]

The theory that existence belongs to that alone which is material necessitates the doctrine of the corporeality of the soul; nor did the Stoics and Epicureans alike shrink from declaring their allegiance to this tenet. Cleanthes and Chrysippus assert it without hesitation.

οὐδὲν ἀσώματον συμπάσχει σώματι οὐδὲ ἀσωμάτῳ σῶμα ἀλλὰ σῶμα σώματι· συμπάσχει δὲ ἡ ψυχὴ τῷ σώματι νοσοῦντι καὶ τεμνομένῳ καὶ τὸ σῶμα τῇ ψυχῇ· αἰσχυνομένης γοῦν ἐρυθρὸν γίνεται καὶ φοβουμένης ὠχρόν. σῶμα ἄρα ἡ ψυχή.[5]

Other Stoic authorities are equally pronounced in this view.

---

[1] *Acad.*, I, 39.
[2] *Comm. Notit.* 30, 2 in Ritter et Preller 396a.
[3] *Diogenes Laertius*, X, 67.
[4] l. 440-8.
[5] Zeller, *Stoics, Epicureans and Sceptics,* 210, 1.

The Epicurean position on this question coincides with that of the Stoics, as the accompanying quotations sufficiently prove.

οἱ λέγοντες ἀσώματον εἶναι τὴν ψυχὴν ματάζουσιν. οὐθὲν γὰρ ἂν ἐδύνατο ποιεῖν οὔτε πάσχειν, εἰ ἦν τοιαύτη· νῦν δ' ἐναγῶς ἀμφότερα ταῦτα συμβαίνει περὶ τὴν ψυχὴν τὰ συμπτώματα.[1]

> *Haec eadem ratio naturam animi atque animai*
> *Corpoream docet esse; ubi enim propellere membra,*
> *Corripere ex somno corpus mutareque vultum*
> *Atque hominem totum regere ac versare videtur,*
> *Quorum nil fieri sine tactu posse videmus*
> *Nec tactum porro sine corpore, nonne fatendumst*
> *Corporea natura animum constare animamque?*[2]

But on the same principles the Stoics proceeded to still greater lengths. They asserted that all properties, qualities and forms were material. Hence, virtues and vices were accounted by them as corporeal, and even emotions, impulses, judgments and notions, which are due to material causes.

ἄτοπον γὰρ εὖ μάλα τὰς ἀρετὰς καὶ τὰς κακίας, πρὸς δὲ ταύταις τὰς τέχνας καὶ τὰς μνήμας πάσας, ἔτι δὲ φαντασίας καὶ πάθη καὶ ὁρμὰς καὶ συγκαταθέσεις σώματα ποιουμένους ἐν μηδενὶ φάναι κεῖσθαι... οἱ δ' οὐ μόνον τὰς ἀρετὰς καὶ τὰς κακίας ζῷα εἶναι λέγουσιν, οὐδὲ τὰ πάθη μόνον, ὀργὰς καὶ φθόνους καὶ λύπας καὶ ἐπιχαιρεκακίας, οὐδὲ καταλήψεις καὶ φαντασίας καὶ ἀγνοίας, οὐδέ τὰς τέχνας ζῷα, τὴν σκυτοτομικὴν τὴν χαλκοτυπικήν, ἀλλὰ πρὸς τούτοις ἔτι καὶ τὰς ἐνεργείας σώματα καὶ ζῷα ποιοῦσι, τόν περίπατον ζῷον, τὴν ὄρχησιν, τὴν ὑπόθεσιν, τὴν προσαγόρευσιν, τὴν λοιδορίαν.[3]

The Good was also regarded by the Stoics as in the same category. Seneca says: *Quaeris, bonum an corpus sit. Bonum facit, prodest enim; quod facit corpus est. · Bonum agitat animum et quodam modo format et continet, quae propria sunt corporis. Quae corporis bona sunt, corpora sunt ergo; et quae animi sunt; nam et hic corpus est. .... Non puto te dubitaturum an adfectus corpora sint,—tanquam ira, amor, tristitia. Si dubitas, vide an voltum nobis mutent, an frontem adstringant, an · faciem diffundant, an ruborem evocent, an fugent sanguinem. Quid ergo, tam manifestas notas corpori credis imprimi nisi a corpore? Si adfectus*

---

[1] *Diogenes Laertius*, X, 67.
[2] III, 161-6.
[3] *Plutarch, Com. Not.*, 45, 2, in Ritter et Preller, 396c.

corpora sunt, et morbi animorum, et avaritia, crudelitas, indurata vitia et in statum inemendabilem adducta; ergo et malitia et species eius omnes, malignitas, invidia, superbia. Ergo et bona, primum quia contraria istis sunt, deinde quia eadem tibi indicia praestabunt.[1]

Truth is likewise placed in the same classification, the significance of truth being the knowledge which the soul possesses in itself.

τὴν δὲ ἀλήθειαν οἴονταί τινες, καὶ μάλιστα οἱ ἀπὸ τῆς Στοᾶς, διαφέρειν τἀληθοῦς κατὰ τρεῖς τρόπους, οὐσίᾳ μὲν παρόσον ἡ μὲν ἀλήθεια σῶμά ἐστι, τὸ δὲ ἀληθὲς ἀσώματον ὑπῆρχεν. καὶ εἰκότως φασίν· τουτὶ μὲν γὰρ ἀξίωμά ἐστι, τὸ δὲ ἀξίωμα λεκτόν, τὸ δὲ λεκτὸν ἀσώματον. ἀνάπαλιν δὲ ἡ ἀλήθεια σῶμά ἐστι παρόσον ἐπιστήμη πάντων ἀληθῶν ἀποφαντικὴ δοκεῖ τυγχάνειν, πᾶσα δὲ ἐπιστήμη πῶς ἔχον ἐστὶν ἡγεμονικόν· τὸ δὲ ἡγεμονικὸν σῶμα κατὰ τούτους ὑπῆρχεν.[2]

Against these and other similar claims of the Stoics, Lucretius opposes his doctrine that there are but two conceivable things in the universe, atoms and the void, *materies et inane*, ἄτομα καὶ κενόν. All other things are not distinct entities, but properties and accidents of things, having no material existence apart from the bodies with which they are identified.

> *Nam quaecumque cluent, aut his coniuncta duabus*
> *Rebus ea invenies aut horum eventa videbis.*
> *Coniunctum est id quod nusquam sine permitiali*
> *Discidio potis est seiungi seque gregari,*
> *Pondus uti saxist, calor ignis, liquor aquai.*
> *Tactus corporibus cunctis intactus inani*
> *Servitium contra paupertas divitiaeque,*
> *Libertas bellum concordia, cetera quorum*
> *Adventu manet incolumis natura abituque,*
> *Haec soliti sumus, ut par est, eventa vocare.*[3]

Starting with the principle that existence alone belongs to that which is material, the Stoics had great difficulty in assigning time and space to their proper category. While they could not describe these as corporeal, they did speak of day and night, months and years and seasons, as bodies, though it is evident that those who did

---

[1] *Epistolae*, 106, 3, in Ritter et Preller, 396C.
[2] *Sext. Math.*, VII, 38, in Ritter et Preller, 396B.
[3] l. 449-59.

so virtually meant that these divisions of time answered to certain material states; the heat of the sun, for example, being responsible for summer, and the other seasons being regulated duly by the approach and retirement of this planet.

τῶν δὲ ἐν ἀέρι γινομένων, χειμῶνα μὲν εἶναι φασὶ τὸν ὑπὲρ γῆς ἀέρα κατεψυγμένον διὰ τὴν τοῦ ἡλίου πρόσω ἄφοδον· ἔαρ δὲ, τὴν εὐκρασίαν τοῦ ἀέρος, κατὰ τὴν πρὸς ἡμᾶς πορείαν.[1]

ἔτι δὲ καὶ τὸν χρόνον ἀσώματον, διάστημα ὄντα τῆς τοῦ κόσμου κινήσεως.[2]

But, while they admitted the incorporeality of time, they insisted on calling it a thing to be regarded by itself like void, though how they reconciled this obvious inconsistency is not recorded. The Epicurean doctrine with reference to time is that it is a particular property of activity and passivity, movement and repose.

οὔτε ἄλλό τι κατ' αὐτοῦ κατηγορητέον ὡς τὴν αὐτὴν οὐσίαν ἔχον τῷ ἰδιώματι τούτῳ (καὶ γὰρ τοῦτο ποιοῦσί τινες), ἀλλὰ μόνον ᾧ συμπλέκομεν τὸ ἴδιον τοῦτο καὶ παραμετροῦμεν, μάλιστα ἐπιλογιστέον. καὶ γὰρ τοῦτο οὐκ ἀποδείξεως προσδεῖται ἀλλ' ἐπιλογισμοῦ, ὅτι ταῖς ἡμέραις καὶ ταῖς νυξὶ συμπλέκομεν καὶ τοῖς τούτων μέρεσιν, ὡσαύτως δὲ καὶ τοῖς πάθεσι καὶ ταῖς ἀπαθείαις, καὶ κινήσεσι καὶ στάσεσιν, ἴδιόν τι σύμπτωμα περὶ ταῦτα πάντα αὐτὸ τοῦτο ἐννοοῦντες, καθ' ὃ χρόνον ὀνομάζομεν.[3]

This more consistent view is well expressed by Lucretius:

> Tempus item per se non est, sed rebus ab ipsis
> Consequitur sensus, transactum quid sit aevo,
> Tum quae res instet, quid porro deinde sequatur.
> Nec per se quemquam tempus sentire fatendumst
> Semotum ab rerum motu placidaque quiete.
>
> . . . . .
>
> Perspicere ut possis res gestas funditus omnis
> Non ita uti corpus per se constare neque esse,
> Nec ratione cluere eadem qua constet inane.
> Sed magis ut merito possis eventa vocare
> Corporis atque loci, res in quo quaeque gerantur.[4]

---

[1] *Diogenes Laertius*, VII, 151.
[2] *Ib.*, 141, Cf., *Sext. Math.*, X, 218, in Ritter et Preller, 399*b*.
[3] *Diogenes Laertius*, X, 72, 73.
[4] I, 459-63; 478-82.

The point of conflict between the two schools in this matter is this,—the Stoics strove very hard to assign corporeality to what the Epicureans described not as being itself, but as modes of being.

In our discussion of Heraclitus we have already adverted to the physical basis with which this philosopher provides the Stoic school by his doctrine of primordial fire. We have also noted the difference of opinion held by critics regarding the real object of Lucretius' attack in the following lines:[1]

> *Quin etiam repetunt a caelo atque ignibus eius,*
> *Et primum faciunt ignem se vertere in auras*
> *Aeris, hinc imbrem gigni, terramque creari*
> *Ex imbri, retroque a terra cuncta reverti,*
> *Umorem primum, post aera, deinde calorem,*
> *Nec cessare haec inter se mutare, meare*
> *A caelo ad terram, de terra ad sidera mundi.*
> *Quod facere haud ullo debent primordia pacto.*
> *Immutabile enim quiddam superare necessest,*
> *Ne res ad nilum redigantur funditus omnes:*
> *Nam quodcumque suis mutatum finibus exit,*
> *Continuo hoc mors est illius quod fuit ante.*
> *Quapropter quoniam quae paulo diximus ante*
> *In commutatum veniunt, constare necessest*
> *Ex aliis ea, quae nequeant convertier usquam,*
> *Ne tibi res redeant ad nilum funditus omnes.*
> *Quin potius tali natura praedita quaedam*
> *Corpora constituas, ignem si forte crearint*
> *Posse eadem, demptis paucis paucisque tributis,*
> *Ordine mutato et motu, facere aeris auras,*
> *Sic alias aliis rebus mutarier omnis?*[2]

Whatever we may determine to have been the actual occasion of this passage, it certainly does not misrepresent the position of the Stoics, if aimed at them. For, observing that warmth supplies nourishment, motion and life to matter, and that heat is existent in all things, they ascribed the origin and preservation of the world to

---

[1] p. 78.
[2] I, 782–802.

fire. Since it is a law of nature that primary being shall transmute itself into specific things, fire passes into air, water, earth; and through the distribution and combination of these elements the world is produced. After describing what, in the Stoic terminology, an element (στοιχείον) signifies, and explaining that Zeno and his followers regarded fire, air, water, earth, as equally essential matter, without any distinctive quality, Diogenes Laertius continues:

ἀνωτάτω μὲν οὖν εἶναι τὸ πῦρ, ὃ δὴ αἰθέρα καλεῖσθαι, ἐν ᾧ πρώτην τὴν τῶν ἀπλανῶν σφαῖραν γεννᾶσθαι, εἶτα τὴν τῶν πλανωμένων· μεθ' ἣν τὸν ἀέρα· εἶτα τὸ ὕδωρ· ὑποστάθμην δὲ πάντων τὴν γῆν, μέσην ἁπάντων οὖσαν.[1]

He also asserts this to be their view of nature:

δοκεῖ δὲ αὐτοῖς τὴν μὲν φύσιν εἶναι πῦρ τεχνικόν, ὁδῷ βαδίζον εἰς γένεσιν, ὅπερ ἐστὶ πνεῦμα πυροειδὲς καὶ τεχνοειδές.[2]

Again on the interchange of the elements, he records the Stoic doctrine as follows:

γίνεσθαι δὲ τὸν κόσμον, ὅταν ἐκ πυρὸς ἡ οὐσία τραπῇ δι' ἀέρος εἰς ὑγρόν, εἶτα τὸ παχυμερὲς αὐτοῦ συστὰν ἀποτελεσθῇ γῆ, τὸ δὲ λεπτομερὲς ἐξαραιωθῇ καὶ τοῦτ' ἐπὶ πλέον λεπτυνθὲν πῦρ ἀπογεννήσῃ· εἶτα κατὰ μῖξιν ἐκ τούων φυτά τε καὶ ζῷα καὶ τὰ ἄλλα γένη.[3]

In a similar strain is the declaration of Plutarch concerning the teaching of Chrysippus:

ἡ δὲ πυρὸς μεταβολή ἐστι τοιαύτη· δι' ἀέρος εἰς ὕδωρ τρέπεται κἀκ τούτου γῆς ὑφισταμένης ἀὴρ ἀναθυμιᾶται· λεπτυνομένου δὲ τοῦ ἀέρος ὁ αἰθὴρ περιχεῖται κύκλῳ, οἱ δ' ἀστέρες ἐκ θαλάσσης μετὰ τοῦ ἡλίου ἀνάπτονται.[4]

The account of the Stoic doctrines contained in Cicero's *De Natura Deorum* coincides with the testimony herewith presented:

Sic enim res habet, ut omnia, quae alantur et quae crescant, contineant in se vim caloris, sine qua neque ali possent nec crescere. Nam omne, quod est calidum et igneum, cietur et agitur motu suo.[5]

Quod quidem Cleanthes his etiam argumentis docet, quanta vis insit

---
[1] VII, 137.
[2] *Ib.*, 156.
[3] *Ib.*, 142.
[4] *Chrysipp. Ap. Plut. Stoic, Rep.* 41, 3, p. 1053, in Ritter et Preller, 405c.
[5] II. 9, 23.

caloris in omni corpore: negat enim esse ullum cibum tam gravem, quin is nocte et die concoquatur; cuius etiam in reliquiis inest calor iis, quas natura respuerit. . . . Omne igitur, quod vivit, sive animal sive terra editum, id vivit propter inclusum in eo colorem. Ex quo intellegi debet eam caloris naturam vim habere in se vitalem per omnem mundum pertinentem.[1]
Et cum quattuor genera sint corporum, vicissitudine eorum mundi continuata natura est. Nam ex terra aqua, ex aqua oritur aer, ex aere aether, deinde retrorsum vicissim ex aethere aer, inde aqua, ex aqua terra infima. Sic naturis his, ex quibus omnia constant sursus deorsus, ultro citro commeantibus mundi partium coniunctio continetur.[2]

The resemblance between the opinions of Heraclitus already noted and the views of the Stoics herein expressed is so close as to imply that whatever Lucretius urges against the doctrine of elemental fire of the one he intends to be valid against the similar doctrine of the other. Both were doubtless in mind as he wrote the passage under consideration. Moreover, whatever he directs against the four elements of Empedocles has a purposed bearing on the physical theories of the Stoics as well.

Lucretius takes issue with the Stoics on the structure and course of the universe no less than on its constituent elements. Having controverted the doctrine of primordial fire, he proceeds to discuss the method by which the universal order came into existence, and finds himself again in conflict with the hereditary foe. Accident, and not design, is responsible for the production of the world. The eternal whirl of the atoms, with their perpetual collisions and attempts at combination, at length succeeded in begetting the present constitution of things. This proposition Lucretius announces repeatedly in the progress of his poem, but never more elaborately than in the following lines:

Nam certe neque consilio primordia rerum
Ordine se suo quaeque sagaci mente locarunt
Nec quos quaeque darent motus pepigere profecto,
Sed quia multa modis multis primordia rerum

---

[1] Cicero, *De Natura Deorum*, II, 9, 24.
[2] *Ib.*, II, 33, 84.

> *Ex infinito iam tempore percita plagis*
> *Ponderibusque suis consuerunt concita ferri*
> *Omnimodisque coire atque omnia pertemptare,*
> *Quae cumque inter se possent congressa creare,*
> *Propterea fit uti magnum volgata per aevom*
> *Omne genus coetus et motus experiundo*
> *Tandem conveniant ea quae convecta repente*
> *Magnarum rerum fiunt exordia semper,*
> *Terrai maris et caeli generisque animantum.*[1]

Such a process of world-formation necessarily involves infinity of matter and of space. Lucretius introduces his argument for this doctrine by a declaration that the universe is infinite, which he illustrates and enforces at some length.

> *Omne quod est igitur nulla regione viarum*
> *Finitumst; namque extremum debebat habere, etc.*[2]

In this he follows Epicurus with remarkable fidelity, both in ideas and phraseology.

τὸ πᾶν ἄπειρόν ἐστι. τὸ γὰρ πεπερασμένον ἄκρον ἔχει· τὸ δὲ ἄκρον παρ' ἕτερόν τι θεωρεῖται. ὥστε οὐκ ἔχον ἄκρον πέρας οὐκ ἔχει· πέρας δὲ οὐκ ἔχον ἄπειρον ἂν εἴη καὶ οὐ πεπρασμένον.[3]

Now, space and matter, being co-extensive with the universe, are also infinite. If space were finite, all matter would sink by gravity to the bottom, whereas we know it is in constant motion.

> *Praeterea spatium summai totius omne*
> *Undique si inclusum certis consisteret oris*
> *Finitumque foret, iam copia materiai*
> *Undique ponderibus solidis confluxet ad imum,*
> *Nec res ulla geri sub caeli tegmine posset,*
> *Nec foret omnino caelum neque lumina solis;*
> *Quippe ubi materies omnis cumulata iaceret*
> *Ex infinito iam tempore subsidendo.*

---

[1] V, 419–31. *Cf.* I, 1021–30; II, 1053–63; V, 187–94.
[2] I, 958–87.
[3] *Diogenes Laertius*, X, 41.

*At nunc, nimirum, requies data principiorum
Corporibus nullast, quia nil est funditus imum,
Quo quasi confluere et sedes ubi ponere possint,
Semper in adsiduo motu res quaeque geruntur
Partibus e cunctis, infernaque suppeditantur
Ex infinito cita corpora materiai.*[1]

But matter must as surely be infinite as space, for the following reasons: It is a provision of nature that Void and Body should bound each other, and these alternations continue to infinity. If space alone were infinite sea, earth, heavens and all the objects of sense would dissolve into ruin. Indeed the atoms would never have combined to form things in beings; nor would the inevitable loss in nature be repaired if there were not an infinite supply of matter. The intricate clashings of the atoms would possibly maintain the unity of the world temporarily, but ultimately disintegration would occur. For the atomic collisions themselves would cease in time without an infinity of matter.[2]

This is the position touching infinity of space and matter which is taken by Epicurus, who says:

καὶ μὴν καὶ τῷ πλήθει τῶν σωμάτων ἄπειρόν ἐστι τὸ πᾶν καὶ τῷ μεγέθει τοῦ κενοῦ. εἴ τε γὰρ ἦν τὸ κενὸν ἄπειρον, τὰ δὲ σώματα ὡρισμένα, οὐδαμοῦ ἂν ἔμενε τὰ σώματα, ἀλλ' ἐφέρετο κατὰ τὸ ἄπειρον κενὸν διεσπαρμένα, οὐκ ἔχοντα τὰ ὑπερείδοντα καὶ στέλλοντα κατὰ τὰς ἀνακοπάς. εἴ τε τὸ κενὸν ἦν ὡρισμένον, οὐκ ἂν εἶχε τὰ ἄπειρα σώματα ὅπου ἐνέστη.[3]

But the Stoic doctrine of the universe is at variance with this. According to Zeno and his followers the earth is a globe resting in the centre of a system known as the world. Immediately above its surface is water, and beyond the water is air. Around these revolves the ether in a circle, composed of several strata, in which are set sun, moon and other heavenly bodies. Beyond this κόσμος is empty space extending to infinity, though the existence of any vacuum within the world is denied.[4] This is the Stoic universe. In such a scheme matter could not be unlimited. The Epicurean conception of the

---

[1] I, 988-1001.
[2] I, 1008-51.
[3] *Diogenes Laertius*, X, 41. 42.
[4] Zeller, *Stoics, Epicureans and Sceptics*, pp. 202, 3.

universe corresponds with that of the Stoics to the extent of regarding the earth as placed in the center of a system enclosed by a circuit of ether studded with celestial spheres. But Epicurus and Lucretius hold this to be but one of an infinite number of worlds, while the Stoics content themselves with a single system and a boundless expanse of space beyond. Epicureanism, therefore, demands an infinite supply of matter for an infinite quantity of worlds, but Stoicism derides the idea of unlimited body, and declares that the very nature of the corporeal renders infinity of matter impossible. The opinions of the Stoic philosophers on this subject are stated by Diogenes Laertius in the following terms:

ἵνα τὸν κόσμον εἶναι καὶ τοῦτον πεπερασμένον, σχῆμα ἔχοντα σφαιροειδές. . ἔξωθεν δ' αὐτοῦ περικεχυμένον εἶναι τὸ κενὸν ἄπειρον, ὅπερ ἀσώματον εἶναι . . . ἐν δὲ τῷ κόσμῳ μηδὲν εἶναι κενόν, ἀλλ' ἡνῶσθαι αὐτόν.[1]
τὸ δὲ πᾶν λέγεται (ὥς φησιν Ἀπολλόδωρος) ὃ δ' τε κόσμος, καὶ καθ' ἕτερον τρόπον τὸ ἐκ τοῦ κόσμου καὶ τοῦ ἔξωθεν κενοῦ, σύστημα. ὁ μὲν οὖν κόσμος πεπερασμένος ἐστί· τὸ δὲ κενόν, ἄπειρον.[2]
σῶμα δέ ἐστι κατ' αὐτοὺς ἡ δ' οὐσία καὶ πεπερασμένη.[3]

But when worlds have once been formed from this infinite supply of matter extending through the universe, how are they held together? This is the question which forces Lucretius into direct conflict with the Stoics, and incidently with the Peripatetics and some other philosophers. The theory of centripetal force as a solution of the problem is scorned by the Epicurean poet.

> *Illud in his rebus longe fuge cedere, Memmi,*
> *In medium summae quod dicunt omnia niti,*
> *Atque ideo mundi naturam stare sine ullis*
> *Ictibus externis neque quoquam posse resolvi*
> *Summa atque ima, quod in medium sint omnia nixa;*
> *Ipsum si quicquam posse in se sistere credis,*
> *Et quae pondera sunt sub terris omnia sursum*
> *Nitier in terraque retro requiescere posta.*[4]

Balbus, who gives an exposition of the Stoic doctrines in Cicero's

---

[1] VII, 140.
[2] *Ib.*, 143.
[3] *Ib.*, 150.
[4] I, 1052-9.

De Natura Deorum, elaborates the exact theory which Lucretius thus condemns.

Omnes enim partes eius undique medium locum capessentes nituntur aequaliter. Maxime autem corpora inter se iuncta permanent, cum quasi quodam vinculo circumdato colligantur; quod facit ea natura, quae per omnem mundum omnia mente et ratione conficiens funditur et ad medium rapit et convertit extrema. . . . Eademque ratione mare, cum supra terram sit, medium tamen terrae locum expetens conglobatur undique aequabiliter neque redundat umquam neque effunditur.[1]

Stobaeus attributes this theory to Zeno.

πάντα τὰ μέρη τοῦ κόσμου ἐπὶ τὸ μέσον τοῦ κόσμου τὴν φορὰν ἔχειν, μάλιστα δὲ τὰ βάρος ἔχοντα.[2]

To Lucretius the conception is absurd, and the existence of the antipodes is ridiculed as the dream of fools.

> *Ut per aquas quae nunc rerum simulacra videmus,*
> *Adsimili ratione animalia suppa vagari*
> *Contendunt, neque posse e terris in loca caeli*
> *Reccidere inferiora magis quam corpora nostra*
> *Sponte sua possint in caeli templa volare*
> *Illi cum videant solem, nos sidera noctis*
> *Cernere, et alternis nobiscum tempora caeli*
> *Dividere et noctes parilis agitare diebus,*
> *Sed vanus stolidis haec* [error somnia finxit].[3]

The inadequacy of the arguments adduced by the Stoics in support of the theory of centripetal force is clearly shown by Lucretius, who denies that infinite space can have any center, and asserts that if it were possible, nothing could come to a rest at this point, since space will always yield to heavy bodies, which cannot lose their weight, in whatever direction they move.[4]

The inconsistency of the Stoics in asserting that only the heavy elements, earth and water, press to the center, while air and fire

---

[1] II, 45, 113, 116.
[2] Munro, II, p. 114.
[3] I, 1060-8.
[4] I, 1069-82.

mount upward, is expressed not only in this connection, but in a subsequent passage, in which Lucretius refutes the Aristotelian notion of an upward centrifugal force.[1] The language of Lucretius is full of force, and justly represents the views of his antagonists.

> *Praeterea quoniam non omnia corpora fingunt*
> *In medium niti, sed terrarum atque liquoris,*
> *Et quasi terreno quae corpore contineantur,*
> *Umorem ponti magnasque e montibus undas,*
> *At contra tenuis exponunt aeris auras*
> *Et calidos simul a medio differrier ignis,*
> *Atque ideo totum circum tremere aethera signis*
> *Et solis flammam per caeli caerula pasci*
> *Quod calor a medio fugiens se ibi contigat omnis,*
> *Nec prorsum arboribus summos frondescere ramos*
> *Posse, nisi a terris paulatim cuique cibatum, etc.*[2]

The teaching of Zeno, as we have sufficient evidence, confirms the charge of incongruity which Lucretius here makes against his followers:

οὐ πάντως δὲ σῶμα βάρος ἔχειν, ἀλλ' ἀβαρῆ εἶναι ἀέρα καὶ πῦρ· γίγνεσθαι δὲ καὶ ταῦτά πως ἐπὶ τὸ τῆς ὅλης σφαίρας τοῦ κόσμου μέσον, τὴν δὲ σύστασιν πρὸς τὴν περιφέρειαν αὐτοῦ ποιεῖσθαι κ.τ.λ.[3]

In has been observed by Munro that "had Epicurus, while retaining his conceptions of infinite space and matter and innumerable worlds and systems, seen fit to adopt this Stoical doctrine of things tending to a center, and so to make his atoms rush from all sides of space alike towards a center, he might have anticipated the doctrine of universal gravity."[4] But he did not possess interest enough in the problems of physical science to pursue them beyond their immediate and obvious relation to ethical questions, nor was his knowledge of mathematics sufficient to lead him toward the discovery which has made the name of Newton immortal. Lucretius, though

---

[1] II, 184-215.
[2] I, 1083-93.
[3] *Stobaeus, Eclogae*, in Munro, II, p. 114.
[4] I, p. 114.

exhibiting keener powers of scientific observation than Epicurus evinces in any fragments of his writings which have been preserved, is in this instance, as in many others, but the echo of his idolized master.

> *Omnis enim locus ac spatium, quod in* [ane vocamus],
> *Per medium, per non medium, concedere* [debet]
> *Aeque ponderibus, motus qua cumque feruntur.*
> *Nec quisquam locus est, quo corpora cum venerunt,*
> *Ponderis amissa vi possint stare in inani:*
> *Nec quod inane autem est ulli subsistere debet,*
> *Quin, sua quod natura petit, concedere pergat.*
> *Haud igitur possunt tali ratione teneri*
> *Res in concilium medii cuppedine vinctae.*[1]

Having shown his hostility to the Stoic conceptions of the origin, constitution and maintenance of the universe, it is natural that Lucretius should oppose the doctrine of the immortality and divinity of the world as held by the followers of Zeno. This he does in the following vigorous protest:

> *Multa tibi expediam doctis solacia dictis;*
> *Religione refrenatus ne forte rearis*
> *Terras et solem et caelum, mare sidera lunam,*
> *Corpore divino debere aeterna manere,*
> *Proptereaque putes ritu par esse Gigantum*
> *Pendere eos poenas inmani pro scelere omnis,*
> *Qui ratione sua disturbent moenia mundi*
> *Praeclarumque velint caeli restinguere solem,*
> *Inmortalia mortali sermone notantes;*
> *Quae procul usque adeo divino a numine distent,*
> *Inque deum numero quae sint indigna videri,*
> *Notitiam potius praebere ut posse putentur*
> *Quid sit vitali motu sensuque remotum.*[2]

While there was apparently some diversity of opinion among the Stoic leaders regarding portions of the doctrine herein assailed,

---

[1] I. 1074-82. *Cf. Diogenes Laertius,* X. 43. 61.
[2] V. 113-25.

there was perfect unanimity touching the identification of the creative energy inherent in primordial fire with deity. The all-pervading essence which was responsible for the world and its phenomena, they argued, could only be defined as the highest reason, operative in matter as the soul is in man. The unity and perfection of the world could only be accounted for on this theory. Nor, without a rational principle acting upon formless matter, could reasoning creatures be produced out of the world. This rational essence, this *anima mundi*, is God. But since, according to the Stoics, deity could only attain reality when clothed with material forms, it was inevitable that the universe and its parts should be regarded as bodying forth divinity, and that ultimately the distinction between the external manifestation and the inner spirit of being should be so obscured as to be practically lost, and the divinity of the world be acknowledged. And this pantheistic conception seems to have prevailed among all the great Stoics except Boethus, who insisted on a separation between God and the world.[1]

Cicero has presented the Stoic view of the divinity of the universe and its parts, and the arguments by which this proposition was sustained with great fulness, as the accompanying excerpts from his elaborate discussion will sufficiently show. To Zeno he attributes these sentiments:

Quod ratione utitur, id melius est quam id, quod ratione non utitur; nihil autem mundo melius; ratione igitur mundus utitur. . . . Nullius sensu carentis pars aliqua potest esse sentiens; mundi autem partes sentientes sunt; non igitur caret sensu mundus. . . . Nihil quod animi quodque rationis est expers, id generare ex se potest animantem conpotemque rationis; mundus autem generat animantis conpotesque rationis; animans est igitur mundus composque rationis. . . . Cur igitur mundus non animans sapiensque iudicetur, cum ex se procreet animantis atque sapientis?[2]

Natura est igitur, quae contineat mundum omnem eumque tueatur, et ea quidem non sine sensu atque ratione; omnem enim naturam necesse est, quae non solitaria sit neque simplex, sed cum alio iuncta atque conexa,

---

[1] Zeller, *Stoics, Epicureans and Sceptics*, pp. 144-160.
[2] *De Natura Deorum*, II. 21, 22.

THE STOICS.

habere aliquem in se principatum. . . . Principatum autem id dico, quod Graeci ἡγεμονικόν *vocant, quo nihil in quoque genere nec potest nec debet esse praestantius. Ita necesse est illud etiam, in quo sit totius naturae principatus, esse omnium optimum omniumque rerum potestate dominatuque dignissimum. Videmus autem in partibus mundi (nihil est enim in omni mundo, quod non pars universi sit) inesse sensum atque rationem. In ea parte igitur, in qua mundi inest principatus, haec inesse necesse est, et acriora quidem atque maiora. Quodcirca sapientem esse mundum necesse est, naturamque eam, quae res omnes conplexa teneat, perfectione rationis excellere, eoque deum esse mundum, omnemque vim mundi natura divina contineri.*[1]

In arguing for the eternal wisdom and virtue of the world the Stoic advocate says:

Si rationis particeps sit nec sit tamen a principio sapiens, non sit deterior mundi potius quam humana condicio; homo enim sapiens fieri potest, mundus autem si in aeterno praeteriti temporis spatio fuit insipiens, nunquam profecto sapientiam consequetur; ita erit homine deterior. Quod quoniam absurdum est, et sapiens a principio mundus et deus habendus est. . . . Est autem nihil mundo perfectius, nihil virtute melius ; igitur mundi est propria virtus. Nec vero hominis natura perfecta est, et efficitur tamen in homine virtus; quanto igitur in mundo facilius. Est ergo in eo virtus; sapiens est igitur et propterea deus.[2]

Diogenes Laertius, in specifying the opinions of Zeno's disciples on the subject under discussion, has the following:

λέγουσι δὲ κόσμον τριχῶς, αὐτόν τε τὸν θεὸν τὸν ἐκ πάσης οὐσίας ἰδίως ποιόν, ὃς δὴ ἄφθαρτός ἐστι καὶ ἀγένητος, δημιουργὸς ὢν τῆς διακοσμήσεως, κατὰ χρόνων ποιὰς περιόδους ἀναλίσκων εἰς ἑαυτὸν τὴν ἅπασαν οὐσίαν καὶ πάλιν ἐξ ἑαυτοῦ γεννῶν.[3]

θεὸν δέ, εἶναι ζῷον ἀθάνατον, λογικὸν,τέλειον, ἢ νοερὸν ἐν εὐδαιμονίᾳ, κακοῦ παντὸς ἀνεπίδεκτον προνοητικὸν κόσμου τε καὶ τῶν ἐν κόσμῳ· μὴ εἶναι μέντοι ἀνθρωπόμορφον. εἶναι δὲ τὸν μὲν, δημιουργὸν τῶν ὅλων, καὶ ὥσπερ πατέρα πάντων· κοινῶς τε καὶ τὸ μέρος αὐτοῦ τὸ διῆκον διὰ πάντων, ὃ πολλαῖς προσηγορίαις προσονομάζεται κατὰ τὰς δυνάμεις.[4]

[1] *De Natura Deorum*, II, 29, 30.
[2] *Ib.*, 36-39.
[3] *Diogenes Laertius*, VII. 137.
[4] *Ib.*, 147.

οὐσίαν δὲ θεοῦ Ζήνων μὲν φησι τὸν ὅλον κόσμον, καὶ τὸν οὐρανόν· ὁμοίως δὲ καὶ Χρύσιππος ἐν τῷ ιά περὶ θεῶν, καὶ Ποσειδώνιος ἐν πρώτῳ περὶ θεῶν.[1]

It is but a step from the acknowledgment of the deity of the world to the acceptance of the divinity of the heavenly bodies which form such an important part of the κόσμος. This the Stoic Balbus avers in Cicero's dissertation on the nature of the gods.[2]

In the same immediate connection is a hearty commendation of Aristotle, whose views on the doctrine under discussion harmonized with the Stoic teaching, and against whom, therefore, together with the Peripatetics, and even Plato, who taught a similar theory, Lucretius, as Munro maintains, evidently directs his shaft.[3]

Because, as has already been demonstrated in the third book of his poem, mind cannot be conceived by him as existing apart from the body, senses and blood, Lucretius insists that the world and its parts cannot be endowed with vitality and intelligence, and is therefore not divine.[4]

But, while this passage seems conclusive against the doctrine of the world as a living organism, it must be acknowledged that Lucretius has been betrayed by his poetic feeling into characterizing the universe in terms which are only appropriate in connection with living beings. Following the analogy of the human body, he has described the world as being produced, increased, wasted and ultimately destroyed like an animal. According to his opinion, it assimilates food, breathes through pores, puts forth herbage corresponding with

---

[1] *Diogenes Laertius*, VII. 148.

[2] *Atque hac mundi divinitate perspecta tribuenda est sideribus eadem divinitas, quae ex mobilissima purissimaque aetheris parte gignuntur, neque ulla praeterea sunt admixta natura totaque sunt calida atque perlucida, ut ea quoque rectissime et animantia esse et sentire atque intellegere dicantur.*—*De Natura Deorum*, II, 39.

οἱ Στωικοὶ . . ἀποφαίνονται . . θεοὺς δὲ καὶ τὸν κόσμον καὶ τοὺς ἀστέρας καὶ τὴν γῆν, τὸν δ᾿ ἀνωτάτω πάντων νοῦν αἰθέρι.—*Plac. I, 7, 33 Dox., 305*, in Ritter et Preller, 398B.

Sensum autem astrorum atque intellegentiam maxume declarat ordo eorum atque constantia. . . . Sequitur ergo, ut ipsa sua sponte, suo sensu ac divinitate moveantur.—*De Natura Deorum*, II. 43.

[3] II, 291.

[4] V. 138-45.

the hair and feathers of animals, begets offspring and exhibits the multiform and varied phenomena of living creatures.[1] Epicurus denounces the doctrine of the divinity of the stars in the following language :

μήτε αὖ πυρὸς ἀνάμματα συνεστραμμένου τὴν μακαριότητα κεκτημένα κατὰ βούλησιν τὰς κινήσεις ταύτας λαμβάνειν.[2] δεῖ κατανοεῖν, ὅτι τάραχος ὁ κυριώτατος ταῖς ἀνθρωπίναις ψυχαῖς γίνεται ἐν τῷ ταῦτα μακάριά τε δοξάζειν (εἶναι) καὶ ἄφθαρτα, καὶ ὑπεναντίας ἔχειν τούτῳ βουλήσεις ἅμα καὶ πράξεις καὶ αἰτίας.[3]

Though Lucretius denies the divinity of the world, he is not so far apart from his philosophic rivals on the question of the world's destructibility as on first observation would appear to be the case. The difference between the Stoic and the Epicurean positions on this subject was due chiefly to the divergence of their respective conceptions of the universe. Zeno and many of his disciples held the theory of recurrent cycles in the career of the world. As matter had in the process of creation been separated from primary being, so eventually it would return to primary being at the end of the present course of things, when a general conflagration would dissolve everything into its primitive elemental condition. As soon as this dissolution had occurred, however, there would begin the formation of a new world exactly conforming in every particular to the preceding one, the identical persons, things and events completing the new cycle which existed in the previous aeon.

ἀρέσκει δ' αὐτοῖς καὶ φθαρτὸν εἶναι τὸν κόσμον, ἅτε γενητὸν τῷ λόγῳ τῶν δι' αἰσθήσεως νοουμένων· οὗ τε τὰ μέρη φθαρτά, ἔστι καὶ τὸ ὅλον· τὰ δὲ μέρη τοῦ κόσμου φθαρτά, εἰς ἄλληλα γὰρ μεταβάλλει· φθαρτὸς ἄρα ὁ κόσμος. καὶ εἴ τι ἐπιδεκτικόν ἐστι τῆς ἐπὶ τὸ χεῖρον μεταβολῆς, φθαρτόν ἐστι· καὶ ὁ κόσμος ἄρα· ἐξαυχμοῦται γὰρ καὶ ἐξυδατοῦται.[4]

Χρύσιππος . . . φησὶν αὔξεσθαι μέχρις ἂν εἰς αὐτὸν ἅπαντα καταναλώσῃ. ἐπεὶ γὰρ ὁ θάνατος μέν ἐστι ψυχῆς χωρισμὸς ἀπὸ τοῦ σώματος, ἡ δὲ τοῦ κόσμου ψυχὴ οὐ χωρίζεται μὲν αὔξεται δὲ συνεχῶς μέχρις ἂν εἰς αὑτὴν ἐξαναλώσῃ τὴν ὕλην, οὐ ῥητέον ἀποθνήσκειν τὸν κόσμον.[5]

---
[1] Cf. II, 1105-74; VI, 492-4; V, 788-91; I, 774. Masson, *Atomic Theory of Lucretius*, pp. 143-9, has a very lucid discussion of this apparent incongruity.
[2] *Diogenes Laertius*, X, 77.
[3] *Ib.*, 81.
[4] *Ib.*, VII, 141.
[5] *Plut. Sto. Rep.*, 39. 2. p. 1052, in Zeller. *Stoics, Epicureans and Sceptics*. p. 164. 2.

While this is the view of the Stoics in the main, several prominent leaders, including Panaetius, Boethus and others, dissented from this judgment. Posidonius is also claimed by Philo as in this class. But Diogenes Laertius, who is confirmed by Plutarch and Stobaeus, asserts that Posidonius believed in the theory of recurrent world-cycles.[1]

The Stoic universe, it must be remembered, however, consisted of the κόσμος, *i. e.*, the world-system of which the earth is the centre, and infinite space. Into this limitless void the κόσμος was dissolved, and from this boundless space it was called together again after each conflagration. In this sense its immortality must be understood. The Epicurean universe, on the other hand, was filled with innumerable worlds or systems, each of which, as it had arisen in time out of the fortuitous concourse of atoms, would also in time wear away and utterly disintegrate into its original and indivisible atoms. But the process of creating worlds anew would continue to infinity, the clashing atoms striking out some fresh order and system as often as by accident the conditions of world formation should be fulfilled. In a way, therefore, the Epicurean τὸ πᾶν is as immortal as the Stoic κόσμος, though the individual world systems of the former are eternally subject to destruction.

Stoicism, it has been remarked, is as much a system of religion as it is a system of philosophy.[2] Theological questions, therefore, occupy a position of pre-eminent importance in its scheme of thought. Moreover, its advocates constantly attempt to harmonize its principles with conventional religion. Epicureanism, on the other hand, treats theology with little less than contempt, and protests against the traditional faith as stultifying to the intellect and pernicious in its influence on character. The Stoic asserts his belief in God on the ground that the existence of the world and the phenomena of life are inexplicable without the hypothesis of an originating and controlling Reason, and because the notion of deity is one of the primary and universal judgments of mankind.[3] The Epicurean,

---

[1] Zeller, *Stoics, Epicureans and Sceptics*, p. 168, 1.
[2] *Ib.*, p. 342.
[3] *Cicero, De Natura Deorum*, II. 4-12.

on the contrary, discerns nothing in nature to indicate the governing presence of the divine, but agrees with the Stoic, though for reasons of his own, that the universal belief in the gods is based on the actual existence of these deities.

Solus enim (Epicurus) vidit primum esse deos, quod in omnium animis eorum notionem impressisset ipsa natura. Quae est enim gens aut quod genus hominum, quod non habeat sine doctrina anticipationem quandam deorum? quam appellat πρόληψιν *Epicurus, id est anticeptam animo rei quandam informationem, sine qua nec intelligi quicquam nec quaeri nec disputari potest.*[1]

That Epicurus believed this πρόληψις to be wrought upon the human consciousness by those emanations, the doctrine of which he borrowed from Empedocles and Democritus, and which have already been considered by us,[2] is amply testified.

Ἐπίκουρος δὲ ἐκ τῶν κατὰ τοὺς ὕπνους φαντασιῶν οἴεται τοὺς ἀνθρώπους ἔννοιαν ἐσπακέναι θεοῦ· μεγάλων γὰρ εἰδώλων, φησί, καὶ ἀνθρωπομόρφων κατὰ τοὺς ὕπνους προσπιπτόντων ὑπέλαβον καὶ ταῖς ἀληθείαις ὑπάρχειν τινὰς τοιούτους θεοὺς ἀνθρωπομόρφους.[3]

Cicero's Epicurean advocate suggests the same:

Nam a natura habemus omnes omnium gentium speciem nullam aliam nisi humanam deorum; quae enim forma alia occurrit umquam aut vigilanti cuiquam aut dormienti? Sed ne omnia revocentur ad primas notiones: ratio hoc idem ipsa declarat.[4]

Lucretius expresses the same theory:

. *de corpore quae sancto simulacra feruntur
In mentes hominum divinae nuntia formae.*[5]

*Quippe etenim iam tum divom mortalia saecla
Egregias animo facies vigilante videbant,
Et magis in somnis mirando corporis auctu.*

---

[1] *Cicero, De Natura Deorum*, I, 43. θεοὶ μὲν γὰρ εἰσίν· ἐναργὴς γὰρ αὐτῶν ἐστιν ἡ γνῶσις. *Diogenes Laertius*, X, 123.

[2] pp. 27, 49, 50.

[3] *Sextus Math. IX, 25*, in Usener *Epicurea*, p. 238.

[4] *De Natura Deorum*. I. 46.

[5] VI, 76, 77.

His igitur sensum tribuebant propterea quod
Membra movere videbantur vocesque superbas
Mittere pro facie praeclara et viribus amplis.
Aeternamque dabant vitam, quia semper eorum
Subpeditabatur facies et forma manebat,
Et tamen omnino quod tantis viribus auctos
Non temere ulla vi convinci posse putabant.
Fortunisque ideo longe praestare putabant,
Quod mortis timor haut quemquam vexaret eorum,
Et simul in somnis quia multa et mira videbant
Efficere et nullum capere ipsos inde laborem.[1]

It has also been conjectured that Epicurus maintained a belief in the gods in order to make possible the realization of the lofty ideals of happiness which he conceived, but which were confessedly never attained in human life.[2]

But the opinions of the character and function of the gods as held by the Stoics and Epicureans respectively were totally at variance. Primary being was conceived of by the Stoics, in one aspect, as the Generative Reason, from which and by which all things are produced. Attention has already been drawn to this tenet.[3] The accompanying quotations likewise support this position:

τοῦτον γὰρ ὄντα ἀΐδιον διὰ πάσης αὐτῆς δημιουργεῖν ἕκαστα.[4]

ἕν τε εἶναι θεὸν καὶ νοῦν, καὶ εἱμαρμένην καὶ Δία, πολλαῖς τε ἑτέραις ὀνομασίαις προσονομάζεσθαι. κατ' ἀρχὰς μὲν οὖν καθ' αὑτὸν ὄντα, τρέπειν τὴν πᾶσαν οὐσίαν δι' ἀέρος εἰς ὕδωρ· καὶ ὥσπερ ἐν τῇ γονῇ τὸ σπέρμα περιέχεται, οὕτω καὶ τοῦτον σπερματικὸν λόγον ὄντα τοῦ κόσμου, τοιόνδε ὑπολιπέσθαι ἐν τῷ ὑγρῷ, εὐεργὸν αὑτῷ ποιοῦντα τὴν ὕλην πρὸς τὴν τῶν ἑξῆς γένεσιν· εἶτα ἀπογεννᾷν πρῶτον τὰ τέσσαρα στοιχεῖα, πῦρ, ὕδωρ, ἀέρα, γῆν.[5]

Δία μὲν γάρ φασι, δι' ὃν τὰ πάντα· Ζῆνα δὲ καλοῦσι, παρ' ὅσον τοῦ ζῆν αἴτιός ἐστιν, ἢ διὰ τοῦ ζῆν κεχώρηκεν· Ἀθηνᾶν δὲ, κατὰ τὴν εἰς αἰθέρα διάτασιν τοῦ ἡγεμονικοῦ αὐτοῦ· Ἥραν δὲ, κατὰ τὴν εἰς τὸ τεχνικὸν πῦρ· καὶ Ποσειδῶνα, κατὰ τὴν εἰς τὸ ὑγρόν· καὶ Δήμητραν, κατὰ τὴν εἰς γῆν· ὁμοίως δὲ καὶ τὰς ἄλλας προσηγορίας, ἐχόμενοί τινος οἰκειότητος, ἀπέδοσαν.[6]

---

[1] V, 1169-82.
[2] Zeller, *Stoics, Epicureans and Sceptics*, p. 466.
[3] *Diogenes Laertius*, VII, 137, quoted p. 99.
[4] *Ib.*, VII, 134.
[5] *Ib.*, 135, 136.
[6] *Ib.*, 147.

It is obvious from these declarations that, while the Stoics in strict consistency assigned the name of Deity in its original significance only to the sole primary Being, "they did not hesitate to apply it in a limited and derivative sense to all those objects by means of which the divine power is especially manifested."[1]

The Epicureans, on the other hand, derided the very idea of the directing presence of deity in the creation, preservation and guidance of the world. The prime purpose of Lucretius, announced at the beginning of his poem and reiterated many times in its progress, is to demonstrate

*et unde queat res quaeque creari
Et quo quaeque modo fiant opera sine divom.*[2]

Velleius, Cicero's exponent of Epicurean principles, ridicules the doctrine of the creation of the world through divine agency, and charges the Stoics with resorting to the hypothesis of gods for lack of any rational method of accounting for the phenomena of nature.

Docuit enim nos idem, qui cetera, natura effectum esse mundum, nihil opus fuisse fabrica, tamque eam rem esse facilem, quam vos effici negatis sine divina posse solertia, ut innumerabilis natura mundos effectura sit, efficiat, effecerit. Quod quia quem ad modum natura efficere sine aliqua mente possit non videtis, ut tragici poetae, cum explicare argumenti exitum non potestis, confugitis ad deum.[3]

The gods of the Epicureans are beings like men, but of a more refined essence. The εἴδωλα of the gods which are presented to our minds, whether asleep or awake, take the figure of men. Moreover, the human form is the most admirable that can be conceived of for rational and happy beings. But divine bodies are not tangible to mortals.

Hominis esse specie deos confitendum est. Nec tamen ea species corpus est, sed quasi corpus, nec habet sanguinem, sed quasi sanguinem.

---

[1] Zeller. *Stoics. Epicureans and Sceptics*, p. 347.
[2] I. 157. 8.
[3] *De Natura Deorum.* I, 53.

... *Epicurus autem, qui res occultas et penitus abditas non modo viderit animo, sed etiam sic tractet, ut manu, docet eam esse vim et naturam deorum, ut primum non sensu, sed mente cernatur; nec soliditate quadam nec ad numerum, ut ea, quae ille propter firmitatem* στερέμνια *appellat, sed imaginibus similitudine et transitione perceptis.*[1]

> *Tenvis enim natura deum longeque remota*
> *Sensibus ab nostris animi vix mente videtur;*
> *Quae quoniam manuum tactum suffugit et ictum,*
> *Tactile nil nobis quod sit contingere debet.*
> *Tangere enim non quit quod tangi non licet ipsum.*[2]

Now, these deities, which are innumerable, are immortal and perfectly happy.

πρῶτον μὲν τὸν θεὸν ζῷον ἄφθαρτον καὶ μακάριον νομίζων, ὡς ἡ κοινὴ τοῦ θεοῦ νόησις ὑπεγράφη, μηθὲν μήτε τῆς ἀφθαρσίας ἀλλότριον μήτε τῆς μακαριότητος ἀνοίκειον αὐτῷ πρόσαπτε· πᾶν δὲ τὸ φυλάττειν αὐτοῦ δυνάμενον τὴν μετὰ ἀφθαρσίας μακαριότητα περὶ αὐτὸν δόξαζε.[3]

τὸ μακάριον καὶ ἄφθαρτον οὔτε αὐτὸ πράγματα ἔχει οὔτε ἄλλῳ παρέχει, ὥστε οὔτε ὀργαῖς οὔτε χάρισι συνέχεται· ἐν ἀσθενεῖ γὰρ πᾶν τὸ τοιοῦτον.[4]

Ea videlicet, qua nihil beatius, nihil omnibus bonis affluentius cogitari potest. Nihil enim agit, nullis occupationibus est implicatus, nulla opera molitur, sua sapientia et virtute gaudet, habet exploratum fore se semper cum in maximis, tum in aeternis voluptatibus.[5]

> *Omnis enim per se divom natura necessest*
> *Inmortali acvo summa cum pace fruatur*
> *Semota ab nostris rebus seiunctaque longe;*
> *Nam privata dolore omni, privata periclis,*
> *Ipsa suis pollens opibus, nil indiga nostri,*
> *Nec bene promeritis capitur neque tangitur ira.*[6]

Their places of abode must also differ from the habitations of men, corresponding in refinement with their bodies.

---

[1] Cicero, *De Natura Deorum*, I, 49.
[2] *Lucretius*, V. 148-52.
[3] *Diogenes Laertius*, X. 123.
[4] *Ib.*, 139, 1.
[5] *De Natura Deorum*, I, 51.
[6] *Lucretius*, II. 646 51.

*Quare etiam sedes quoque nostris sedibus esse
Dissimiles debent, tenues de corpore eorum.*[1]

*Apparet divum numen sedesque quietae
Quas neque concutiunt venti nec nubila nimbis
Aspergunt neque nix acri concreta pruina
Cana cadens violat semperque innubilis aether
Integit, et large diffuso lumine rident.
Omnia suppeditat porro natura neque ulla
Res animi pacem delibat tempore in ullo.*[2]

Gods, however, it is easy to observe, who have the amount of business on their hands which the Stoics attribute to their deities, must be far from happy, so Epicurus and his disciples would contend.

οὐ γὰρ συμφωνοῦσιν πραγματεῖαι καὶ φροντίδες καὶ ὀργαὶ καὶ χάριτες μακαριότητι, ἀλλ' ἐν ἀσθενείᾳ καὶ φόβῳ καὶ προσδεήσει τῶν πλησίον ταῦτα γίνεται.[3] καὶ ἡ θεία φύσις πρὸς ταῦτα μηδαμῇ προσαγέσθω, ἀλλ' ἀλειτούργητος διατηρείσθω καὶ ἐν τῇ πάσῃ μακαριότητι.[4]

The Epicurean Velleius indulges in merriment over the Stoic notion of the world as a divinity, eternally revolving in space with inevitable discomfort, and seriously combats their favorite doctrine of Providence on the ground that such constant occupation would be destructive of the peace and quietude which are indispensable in his opinion to the complete happiness of the gods.

Sive in ipso mundo deus inest aliquis, qui regat, qui gubernet, qui cursus astrorum, mutationes temporum, rerum vicissitudines ordinesque conservet, terras et maria contemplans hominum commoda vitasque tueatur, ne ille est implicatus molestis negotiis et operosis! Nos autem beatam vitam in animi securitate et in omnium vacatione munerum ponimus.[5]

We have already seen how necessary to the happiness of the gods Lucretius regards their total exemption from the cares of government.

---

[1] V, 153, 4.
[2] III, 18-24.
[3] *Diogenes Laertius*, X. 77.
[4] *Ib.*, 97.
[5] *De Natura Deorum*, I. 52, 53.

But the providence of the gods is a doctrine to which the Stoics adhered with extraordinary tenacity. It was esteemed fundamental in their system of philosophy.

τὸν δὴ κόσμον διοικεῖσθαι κατὰ νοῦν καὶ πρόνοιαν. . . . εἰς ἅπαν αὐτοῦ μέρος διήκοντος τοῦ νοῦ, καθάπερ ἐφ' ἡμῶν τῆς ψυχῆς. . . . οὕτω δὴ καὶ τὸν ὅλον κόσμον ζῷον ὄντα καὶ ἔμψυχον καὶ λογικὸν ἔχειν ἡγεμονικὸν μὲν τὸν αἰθέρα, κ. τ. λ.[1] λέγει γοῦν Χρύσιππος ἐοικέναι τῷ μὲν ἀνθρώπῳ τὸν Δία καὶ τὸν κόσμον, τῇ δὲ ψυχῇ τὴν πρόνοιαν· ὅταν οὖν ἐκπύρωσις γένηται, μόνον ἄφθαρτον ὄντα τὸν Δία τῶν θεῶν ἀναχωρεῖν ἐπὶ τὴν πρόνοιαν, εἶτα ὁμοῦ γενομένους ἐπὶ μιᾶς τῆς τοῦ αἰθέρος οὐσίας διατελεῖν ἀμφοτέρους.[2]

The Stoic Balbus presents the arguments of his school in defence of the doctrine of the providence of the gods in a three-fold arrangement, as follows: First, if we admit the existence of gods, we must grant that they govern the world, otherwise they would not deserve the title of deities; for the very conception of gods implies that they are independent of all power other than their own, and that they work together harmoniously and wisely for the noblest end, which is nothing less than the government of the world. Second, the order and unity of the universe indicate that all its parts are under the control of a force working intelligently and skillfully, which we denominate Nature. But it is impossible for a thinking man to examine this orderly course of the world without being convinced that it is under the direction of a wise mind. Third, the regularity, harmony and beauty of the heavenly bodies; the constitution, endowments and wondrous adaptations of plants and animals; and the various productions of the earth, suited so remarkably to the need of living creatures, all unite to confirm the wise man in his belief in a divine providence.[3] Based on the most reliable extant authorities, Zeller has formulated the Stoic arguments for this doctrine in this order: (1) From the general conviction of mankind. (2) From the perfection of God. (3) From the theory of necessity. (4) From the foreknowledge of God. (5) From the existence of divination.[4]

---

[1] *Diogenes Laertius*, VII. 138, 139.
[2] *Plutarch. De Comm. Notit.*: 36, 5. p. 1077, in Ritter et Preller, 401 B.
[3] *De Natura Deorum*, II. 75-152.
[4] *Stoics, Epicureans and Sceptics*, pp. 173-75.

Perhaps the finest expression of the Stoic belief in the guidance of God which has been preserved for us is contained in the famous *Hymn to Zeus* by Cleanthes, a portion of which we quote.

κύδιστ' ἀθανάτων, πολυώνυμε, παγκρατὲς αἰεί,
Ζεῦ, φύσεως ἀρχηγέ, νόμου μέτα πάντα κυβερνῶν,
χαῖρε· σὲ γὰρ πάντεσσι θέμις θνητοῖσι προσαυδᾶν.
ἐκ σοῦ γὰρ γένος ἐσμέν, ἰῆς μίμημα λαχόντες
μοῦνοι, ὅσα ζώει τε καὶ ἕρπει θνήτ' ἐπὶ γαῖαν.
τῷ σε καθυμνήσω, καὶ σὸν κράτος αἰὲν ἀείσω.
σοὶ δὴ πᾶς ὅδε κόσμος, ἑλισσόμενος περὶ γαῖαν
πείθεται ᾗ κεν ἄγῃς καὶ ἑκὼν ὑπὸ σεῖο κρατεῖται.
τοῖον ἔχεις ὑποεργὸν ἀκινήτοις ἐνὶ χερσίν,
ἀμφήκη, πυρόεντα, ἀεὶ ζώοντα κεραυνόν,
τοῦ γὰρ ὑπὸ πληγῆς φύσεως πάντ' ἐρρίγασιν.

. . . .

οὐδέ τι γίγνεται ἔργον ἐπὶ χθονὶ σοῦ δίχα, δαῖμον,
οὔτε κατ' αἰθέριον θεῖον πόλον, οὔτ' ἐπὶ πόντῳ,
πλὴν ὁπόσα ῥέζουσι κακοὶ σφετέρῃσιν ἀνοίαις.
ἀλλὰ σὺ καὶ τὰ περισσὰ ἐπίστασαι ἄρτια θεῖναι,
καὶ κοσμεῖς τὰ ἄκοσμα, καὶ οὐ φίλα σοὶ φίλα ἐστίν.
ὦδε γὰρ εἰς ἓν ἅπαντα συνήρμοκας ἐσθλὰ κακοῖσιν,
ὥσθ' ἓν γίγνεσθαι πάντων λόγον αἰὲν ἐόντα.[1]

The whole teaching of these noble verses is utterly repugnant to the theology of the Epicureans, who not only deem the labor of ruling the world incompatible with the unquestioned happiness of the gods, but who profess to see nothing in the adjustments of nature or the experience of men to justify a belief in the providence of the gods. One of the chief reasons for the Stoic confidence in the existence and guardianship of the gods lies in the perfection of the world which they allege, but which the Epicureans strenuously deny.

Quid autem est inscitius quam eam naturam, quae omnis res sit conplexa, non optumam dici. . . . Neque enim est quicquam aliud praeter mundum, cui nihil absit, quodque undique aptum atque perfectum expletumque sit omnibus suis numeris et partibus.[2]

---

[1] *Stobaeus Eclogae.*, I, p. 30.
[2] Cicero, *De Natura Deorum*, II, 36, 37.

Lucretius can discover no warrant in nature for such a view. On the contrary, he finds such palpable imperfections in creation that if he were totally ignorant of the true philosophy of the universe he would still never hesitate to condemn the notion that the world was constructed by divine power.

> *Nam quamvis rerum ignorem primordia quae sint,*
> *Hoc tamen ex ipsis caeli rationibus ausim*
> *Confirmare aliisque ex rebus reddere multis,*
> *Nequaquam nobis divinitus esse creatam*
> *Naturam mundi: tanta stat praedita culpa.*[1]

The argument by which Lucretius sustains his opinion is interesting, if not convincing. The defect of nature is apparent in the immense waste of the world as compared with its productive portions. Even where tillage is possible with almost incredible labor, the toil of the husbandman is frequently thrown away, for thorns infest the soil, and burning heat, chilling blasts and destructive hurricanes defeat the projects of the farmer. Again, man himself is beset with constant perils. Ferocious beasts roam abroad. Disease and death walk in the train of the seasons. Helpless infancy is dependent on the care of elders, while the young of animals flourish attended only by the bounty of nature.[2]

There is an uncertainty and capriciousness also about the operation of some of the forces of nature, not to speak of the impossibility that any personal agency should control these forms of energy, which prevents him from believing the gods maintain any active interest in the progress of human affairs.

> *Quae bene cognita si teneas, natura videtur*
> *Libera continuo, dominis privata superbis,*
> *Ipsa sua per se sponte omnia dis agere expers.*
> *Nam pro, sancta deum tranquilla pectora pace*
> *Quae placidum degunt aevom vitamque serenam,*
> *Quis regere immensi summam, quis habere profundi*
> *Indu manu validas potis est moderanter habenas,*

---

[1] II, 177–81.
[2] V, 195–234.

Quis pariter caelos omnis convertere et omnis
Ignibus aetheriis terras suffire feracis,
Omnibus inve locis esse omni tempore praesto,
Nubibus ut tenebras faciat caelique serena
Concutiat sonitu, tum fulmina mittat et aedis
Saepe suas disturbet et in deserta recedens
Saeviat, exercens telum, quod saepe nocentes
Praeterit exanimatque indignos inque merentes?[1]

The real animus of the Epicurean eagerness to disprove the providence of the gods lies, of course, in the purpose to deliver men from the fear of deity, which Lucretius and his school felt to be incident to a belief in this doctrine.

Nam et praestans deorum natura hominum pietate coleretur, cum et aeterna esset et beatissima (habet enim venerationem iustam, quicquid excellit), et metus omnis a vi atque ira deorum pulsus esset; intellegitur enim a beata inmortalique natura et iram et gratiam segregari; quibus remotis nullos a superis impendere metus.[2]

The supreme inspiration of Lucretius' philosophical inquiries is the desire to deliver men from the dread of divine malevolence. His passion for the redemption of mankind from irrational terrors is exceedingly impressive. He bewails the puerile credulity of the race.

Nam veluti pueri trepidant atque omnia caecis
In tenebris metuunt, sic nos in luce timemus
Interdum, nilo quae sunt metuenda magis quam
Quae pueri in tenebris pavitant finguntque futura.[3]

He would dispel such groundless forebodings by means of the revelations of true science.

Hunc igitur terrorem animi tenebrasque necessest
Non radii solis neque lucida tela diei
Discutiant, sed naturae species ratioque.[4]

---
[1] II, 1090-1104.
[2] *De Natura Deorum*, I, 45.
[3] II, 55-58.
[4] V, 1211-17.

It is lack of knowledge which betrays men into misinterpretations of the phenomena of nature, and impels them to cringe before the gods as if they were the relentless enemies of mankind. We observe the wondrous movements of the celestial bodies, and are incapable of solving the problems of their regularity and persistence, and profound misgivings are awakened.

> *Temptat enim dubiam mentem rationis egestas,*
> *Ecquaenam fuerit mundi genitalis origo,*
> *Et simul ecquae sit finis, quoad moenia mundi*
> *Solliciti motus hunc possint ferre laborem,*
> *An divinitus aeterna donata salute*
> *Perpetuo possint aevi labentia tractu*
> *Immensi validas aevi contemnere viris.* [1]

The vivid lightnings and the noisy thunder terrify monarchs and people with the expectation of merited retribution. The tempestuous sea mocks the skill and defies the prayers of the mariner. The mysterious earthquake tumbles down the proudest works of man, while he, unable to account for these disasters on natural grounds, attributes them to the wrath of the gods.[2]

> *O genus infelix humanum, talia divis*
> *Cum tribuit facta atque iras adiunxit acerbas!*
> *Quantos tum gemitus ipsi sibi, quantaque nobis*
> *Volnera, quas lacrimas pepercre minoribu' nostris!*[3]

A better philosophy, Lucretius believes, would emancipate humanity from the grasp of such a foolish trepidation; and with this in view he devotes the entire sixth book of his poem to the consideration of the physical phenomena which appall the senses. When men, for the want of the true reason of things, assign fear-inducing operations of nature to the activity of the gods, Lucretius feels that they are stultifying both themselves and the deities whom they seek to propitiate.

---

[1] V, 1211-17.
[2] V, 1218-40.
[3] V, 1194-97.

*Nam bene qui didicere deos securum agere aevom,
Si tamen interea mirantur qua ratione
Quaeque geri possint, praesertim rebus in illis
Quae supera caput aetheriis cernuntur in oris,
Rursus in antiquas referuntur religionis,
Et dominos acris adsciscunt, omnia posse
Quos miseri credunt, ignari quid queat esse,
Quid nequeat, finita potestas denique cuique
Quanam sit ratione atque alte terminus haerens;
Quo magis errantes caeca ratione feruntur.
Quae nisi respuis ex animo longeque remittis
Dis indigna putare alienaque pacis eorum,
Delibata deum per te tibi numina sancta
Saepe oberunt; non quo violari summa deum vis
Possit, ut ex ira poenas petere inbibat acris,
Sed quia tute tibi placida cum pace quietos
Constitues magnos irarum volvere fluctus,
Nec delubra deum placido cum pectore adibis,
Nec de corpore quae sancto simulacra feruntur
In mentes hominum divinae nuntia formae,
Suscipere haec animi tranquilla pace valebis.
Inde videre licet qualis iam vita sequatur.*[1]

Almost the only occasion for scientific study which Lucretius would deem legitimate is the necessity of showing by this kind of research that the things which terrify man in the external universe have a natural rather than a divine origin. And this is the reason which Epicurus himself gives for his investigations in the realm of physics. Men can never realize even approximate happiness until their bondage to superstition has been broken, a result which an inquiry into the processes of nature will achieve.

εἰ μηθὲν ἡμᾶς αἱ τῶν μετεώρων ὑποψίαι ἠνώχλουν καὶ αἱ περὶ θανάτου, μή ποτε πρὸς ἡμᾶς ᾖ τι, ἔτι τε τὸ μὴ κατανοεῖν τοὺς ὅρους τῶν ἀλγηδόνων καὶ τῶν ἐπιθυμιῶν, οὐκ ἂν προσεδεόμεθα φυσιολογίας.[2]

It is characteristic of Lucretius that after a lengthy disquisition on

---

[1] VI, 56-74.
[2] *Diogenes Laertius*, X, 142.

the natural philosophy of thunderbolts he should turn with vehemence upon the traditional mode of accounting for the ravages of lightning, and endeavor to reduce the theory to utter absurdity. It is folly, he says, to consult the Tuscan rolls to ascertain the will of the gods in the thunderbolt's erratic course. If Jupiter controls the lightning why does he frequently smite the innocent instead of the guilty? Why does he direct his fiery bolts at solitary places on the earth? Why fling them into the sea? Why does he not warn us if he wishes us to escape the destructive agent? Why does he thunder if he wishes to take us off our guard? How can he hurl his shafts in so many different places at one time? Why does he thunder only when the sky is overclouded? Above all, why does Jupiter dash down his own sanctuaries and the cunningly wrought idols of the gods, and why does he aim chiefly at lofty summits?[1]

In arguing for the existence and providence of the gods, the Stoics placed much reliance on their doctrine of final causes. The subordination of means to ends was to them an obvious fact in all the minute details of the world's career. Cleanthes supported his argument for the existence of the gods by this form of proof, the most significant of his utterances on this subject being:

Ut, si quis in domum aliquam aut in gymnasium aut in forum venerit, cum videat omnium rerum rationem, modum, disciplinam, non possit ea sine causa fieri iudicare, sed esse aliquem intellegat, qui praesit et cui pareatur, multo magis in tantis motionibus tantisque vicissitudinibus, tam multarum rerum atque tantarum ordinibus, in quibus nihil umquam inmensa et infinita vetustas mentita sit, statuat necesse est ab aliqua mente tantos naturae motus gubernari.[2]

The argument for providence is as pertinent as that for the existence of the gods:

Namque alii naturam esse censent vim quandam sine ratione cientem motus in corporibus necessarios, alii autem vim participem rationis atque ordinis tamquam via progredientem declarantemque, quid cuiusque rei causa efficiat, quid sequatur, cuius sollertiam nulla ars, nulla manus, nemo opifex consequi possit imitando; seminis enim vim esse tantam, ut id,

---

[1] VI, 379-422.
[2] Cicero, *De Natura Deorum*, II, 5, 15.

quamquam sit perexiguum, tamen, si inciderit in concipientem conprendentemque naturam nanctumque sit materiam, qua ali augerique possit, ita fingat et efficiat in suo quidque genere.[1]

With the Stoics the adapting of means to ends signified that everything had been created for something higher, except man and the gods, who existed for their own society:

Scite enim Chrysippus, ut clipei causa involucrum, vaginam autem gladii, sic praeter mundum cetera omnia aliorum causa esse generata, ut eas fruges atque fructus, quos terra gignit, animantium causa, animantes autem hominum, ut equum vehendi causa, arandi bovem, venandi et custodiendi canem. Ipse autem homo ortus est ad mundum contemplandum et imitandum, nullo modo perfectus, sed est quaedam particula perfecti.[2] *Praeclare enim Chrysippus, cetera nata esse hominum causa et deorum, eos autem communitatis et societatis suae.*[3]

Naturally a system of philosophy which refers all phenomena to accidental causes would spurn any teleological theory. Accordingly we find Lucretius saying:

> *Dicere porro hominum causa voluisse parare*
> *Praeclaram mundi naturam proptereaque*
> *Adlaudabile opus divom laudare decere*
> *Aeternumque putare atque immortale futurum*
> *Nec fas esse, deum quod sit ratione vetusta*
> *Gentibus humanis fundatum perpetuo aevo,*
> *Solicitare suis ulla vi ex sedibus umquam*
> *Nec verbis vexare et ab imo evertere summa,*
> *Cetera de genere hoc adfingere et addere, Memmi,*
> *Desiperest.*[4]

Cicero's Epicurean expositor presents what he evidently regards an insoluble dilemma:

---

[1] *De Natura Deorum*, II, 32, 81, 82.
[2] *Ib.*, 14, 37.
[3] *De Finibus*, III, 20, 67.
[4] V, 156-165.

An haec, ut fere dicitis, hominum causa a deo constituta sunt? Sapientiumque? Propter paucos igitur tanta est facta rerum molitio. An stultorum? At primum causa non fuit, cur de inprobis bene mereretur, etc.[1]

To impose upon the gods, moreover, the premeditation involved in adapting the processes of nature to definite ends would be incompatible with their happiness. What could induce them to assume such burdens? What injury should we have suffered if we had never been born? Whence did the gods derive their conception of man in order to create him?[2] These are questions which Lucretius answers by denying the participation of the gods in mundane affairs, and by re-asserting his favorite thesis of the fortuitous concourse of atoms.

> *Namque ita multa modis multis primordia rerum*
> *Ex infinito iam tempore percita plagis*
> *Ponderibusque suis consuerunt concita ferri*
> *Omnimodisque coire atque omnia pertemptare,*
> *Quaecumque inter se possent congressa creare,*
> *Ut non sit mirum, si in talis dispositusas*
> *Deciderunt quoque et in talis venere meatus,*
> *Qualibus haec rerum geritur nunc summa novando.*[3]

Again, he asserts in the most unequivocal language his hostility to the doctrine that the functions of the body were originally created for the uses to which they have been placed. Experience, on the contrary, taught the use of these organs long after they had been constructed. Appliances of war and peace were invented for definite purposes, but the senses and limbs of the human body, unlike swords, shields, cups and beds, were created without any final cause.

> *Nil ideo quoniam natumst in corpore ut uti*
> *Possemus, sed quod natumst id procreat usum.*[4]

---

[1] *De Natura Deorum*, I, 23.
[2] V, 166-86.
[3] *Ib.*, 187-194.
[4] IV, 823-57.

But while the Epicureans denounced the doctrine of divine providence, they were not averse to a dispassionate veneration of the gods. The existence of deities they could not deny without being false, as we have seen, to their principle that every impression of the soul has its origin in objective reality. Deficient of any power to interfere in the affairs of men, the gods were nevertheless to be adored as beings of purity, holiness and eternal peace. Epicurus himself is praised for his piety.

τῆς μὲν γὰρ πρὸς θεοὺς ὁσιότητος καὶ πρὸς πατρίδα φιλίας ἄλεκτος ἡ διάθεσις.[1]

His followers did not disdain to engage in religious ceremonies, and Cicero declares that, while Epicureans were hostile to traditional religion in theory, they were in repeated instances distinctly superstitious.

Novi ego Epicureos omnia sigilla venerantes; quamquam video non nullis videri Epicurum, ne in offensionem Atheniensium caderet, verbis reliquisse deos, re sustulisse.[2]

In the elaborate and truly poetic phrasing of the myth of Kybele Lucretius appears to lend some countenance to the popular religion. But he is not a sincere expositor of the theology of the people, but a satirist, parodying the mode of accommodating physical facts to the traditional mythology of the ancient Greeks adopted by the Stoics. This is apparent from the declaration at the end of the passage:

---

[1] *Diogenes Laertius*, X, 10.
[2] *De Natura Deorum*, I, 85. We have trustworthy evidence that Cicero, who has so fully presented the Epicurean case against the Stoics, derived his materials directly from Philodemus. From the legible remnants of this teacher found in the *Volumina Herculanensia*, it becomes quite apparent 'that Cicero took the body of Φιλοδήμου περὶ εὐσεβείας, and appropriated it to his own uses. Mayor (*De Natura Deorum, Introduction, pp. XLIII, LIII.*) has given a strong putting of the case, from which we abridge the following points of resemblance between Cicero and Philodemus: 1. Particular citations from the writings of opponents, such as Xenophon, Antisthenes, Aristotle, Chrysippus, Diogenes of Babylon. 2. Divisions of the two documents. (*a*) Criticism of popular mythology. (*b*) Criticism of the older philosophers. (*c*) Exposition of Epicurean theology. 3. Similar lists in Cicero and Philodemus of philosophers, following much the same order. These are arranged in parallel columns by Diels (*Doxographi Graeci, pp. 531–50*), and afford a striking confirmation of the theory that Cicero used Philodemus freely.

*Hic siquis mare Neptunum Cereremque vocare
Constituit fruges et Bacchi nomine abuti
Mavolt quam laticis proprium proferre vocamen,
Concedamus ut hic terrarum dictitet orbem
Esse deum matrem, dum vera re tamen ipse
Religione animum turpi contingere parcat.*[1]

The true animus of Lucretius is seen in the lines immediately preceding, in which he proclaims the doctrine of the happiness and supreme repose of the gods, who rest in blissful security unmoved by the prayers and miseries of mankind.[2] The absurd length to which the Stoics carried their method of allegorical interpretation, an ample illustration of which we have in Cicero's exposition of the subject,[3] justified the warmth of Lucretius' satire. For with an elasticity, which to a man as earnest as Lucretius seemed insincerity, the Stoics in a derivative sense invested with the prerogatives of deity stars, years, months, seasons, air, earth, fire, water, fruits, wine, etc., then great heroes, and finally the very qualities which dignify spiritual beings, hope, truth, freedom, honor, virtue, justice, love, etc. With marvellous facility, therefore, Stoicism could assimilate to itself the conceptions of conventional polytheism. The Epicurean, on the other hand, was willing to give a poetic interpretation to the anthropomorphic ideas of the people, and by reason of his assumption of innumerable gods, was able to bring himself into sympathetic relations with persons adhering to the traditional cult, while at the same time he successfully undermined the whole scheme of the popular religion by his rationalistic explanations. Lucretius consents to call the earth the mother of the gods, and, as we have seen, permits the names Neptune, Ceres, Bacchus, to be employed for the sea, corn and wine. But he emphatically asserts that Epicurus, whose philosophy emancipates men from superstition, is more deserving of divine honors than Ceres, Liber and Hercules, the last mentioned being especially revered by the Stoics.[4]

---

[1] II, 652-7.
[2] II, 646-51.
[3] *De Natura Deorum*, II, 40-44; 59-70.
[4] V, 1-54.

The popular faith was supported by the Stoics on account of its practical value. It constituted in their judgment an effective check to the evil passions of humanity. But Epicureans regarded the traditional religion as vicious in its influence upon character. The pernicious ethical results of the prevalent superstition touching the gods evoked the bitterest hostility of Lucretius. The cowardice, sycophancy and crime which the fear of deity engendered were sufficient, he felt, to condemn the accepted theology. With a passionate earnestness which is born of his enthusiasm for humanity he smites with terrific energy the false-hearted zeal which would destroy innocent life to appease the wrath of jealous gods. The tragic story of the sacrifice of Iphigeneia rouses him to a fury of denunciation.[1] It is impossible not to sympathize with his hatred of a religion that could engender such wrongs. Impiety does not consist, as he declares, in rejecting but in respecting such a faith.

> *Nec pietas ullast velatum saepe videri*
> *Vertier ad lapidem atque omnis accedere ad aras,*
> *Nec procumbere humi prostratum et pandere palmas*
> *Ante deum delubra, nec aras sanguine multo*
> *Spargere quadrupedum, nec votis nectere vota,*
> *Sed mage pacata posse omnia mente tueri.*[2]

And this sentiment Epicurus expresses with great clearness:

ἀσεβὴς δὲ οὐχ ὁ τοὺς τῶν πολλῶν θεοὺς ἀναιρῶν, ἀλλ' ὁ τὰς τῶν πολλῶν δόξας θεοῖς προσάπτων.[3]

It may not be amiss, however, to observe that the invocation of a popular deity at the beginning of his poem[4] by one who so fiercely assails conventional religion is an apparent incongruity, to explain which has taxed the ingenuity of the acutest critics.

The ethical purpose of the Stoic was practically identical with that of the Epicurean. Consequently Lucretius finds little occasion of conflict with his chief philosophic rivals on this score. He does,

---
[1] I, 80–101.
[2] V, 1196–1201.
[3] *Diogenes Laertius*, X. 123.
[4] I, 1–40.

however, arraign the followers of Zeno somewhat sharply on the ground of their doctrine of the apathy of the wise man. Stoicism required the utter suppression of the emotions for the attainment of virtue. Ideally the wise man is devoid of anger, fear, envy, shame, care, pity; he is exempt from all passions, appetites, enthusiasms. Emotions are perturbations of mental equilibrium. If permitted to continue they finally develop into incurable diseases of the soul.[1] The wise man, therefore, must be simply emotionless. Virtue is apathy. φασὶ δὲ καὶ ἀπαθῆ εἶναι τὸν σοφὸν, διὰ τὸ ἀνέμπτωτον.[2] Right reason, which is another name for philosophy, will enable men to reach this estate. With such teaching Lucretius takes issue. Reason, he admits, will achieve much, but it will never altogether obliterate a man's distinctive characteristics.

> Sic hominum genus est. Quamvis doctrina politos
> Constituat pariter quosdam, tamen illa relinquit
> Naturae cuiusque animi vestigia prima.
> Nec radicitus evelli mala posse putandumst,
> Quin proclivius hic iras decurrat ad acris,
> Ille metu citius paulo templetur, at ille
> Tertius accipiat quaedam clementius aequo.
> Inque aliis rebus multis differe necessest
> Naturas hominum varias moresque sequacis;
> Quorum ego nunc nequeo caecas exponere causas,
> Nec reperire figuratum tot nomina quot sunt
> Principiis, unde haec oritur variantia rerum.[3]

At the same time a life truly god-like is possible to the philosopher. So taught Epicurus, the master.

ταῦτα οὖν καὶ τὰ τούτοις συγγενῆ μελέτα πρὸς σεαυτὸν ἡμέρας καὶ νυκτὸς πρός [τε] τὸν ὅμοιον σεαυτῷ, καὶ οὐδέποτε οὔθ' ὕπαρ οὔτ' ὄναρ διαταραχθήσῃ, ζήσεις δὲ ὡς θεὸς ἐν ἀνθρώποις. οὐθὲν γὰρ ἔοικε θνητῷ ζῴῳ ζῶν ἄνθρωπος ἐν ἀθανάτοις ἀγαθοῖς.[4]

---

[1] *Diogenes Laertius*, VII, 115.
[2] *Ib.*, 117.
[3] III, 307-18.
[4] *Diogenes Laertius*, X, 135.

So believed Lucretius the disciple.

> *Illud in his rebus videor firmare potesse,*
> *Usque adeo naturarum vestigia linqui*
> *Parvola, quae nequeat ratio depellere nobis,*
> *Ut nil inpediat dignam dis degere vitam.*[1]

THE END.

---

[1] III, 319-22.

www.ingramcontent.com/pod-product-compliance
Lightning Source LLC
Chambersburg PA
CBHW020124170426
43199CB00009B/625